Flowers of Cuba

Caribbean Pocket Natural History

Flowers of Cuba

Angela T. Leiva Sánchez
Translated by Juliet Barclay
Photography by Gonzalo Canetti

MACMILLAN
CARIBBEAN

Macmillan Education
Between Towns Road, Oxford, OX4 3PP
A division of Macmillan Publishers Limited
Companies and representatives throughout the world

www.macmillan-caribbean.com

ISBN: 978-1-4050-2904-9

Text © Angela T. Leiva Sánchez 2007
Design and illustration © Macmillan Publishers Limited 2007

First published 2007

All rights reserved; no part of this publication may be reproduced, stored in a retrieval system, transmitted in any form or by any means, electronic, mechanical, photocopying, recording, or otherwise, without the prior written permission of the publishers.

Designed by Carol Hulme
Typeset by CjB Editorial Plus
Map by Tek-Art
Cover design by Gary Fielder
Cover photographs by Gonzalo Canetti

Commissioned photographs by Gonzalo Canetti

All photographs were taken by Gonzalo Canetti except for pp. 9 (b), 10, 24 (b), 30 (b), 35, 40, 42, 72, 76 (b) and 101 by Monica Warner, and pp. 17 and 51 by Sean Carrington.

Printed and bound in Malaysia

2011 2010 2009 2008 2007
10 9 8 7 6 5 4 3 2 1

Contents

Map of Cuba	vi
Introduction	vii
The Flowers 　　Descriptive text and photographs	1
Glossary	104
Bibliography	105
Index of Common Names	107
Index of Scientific Names	111

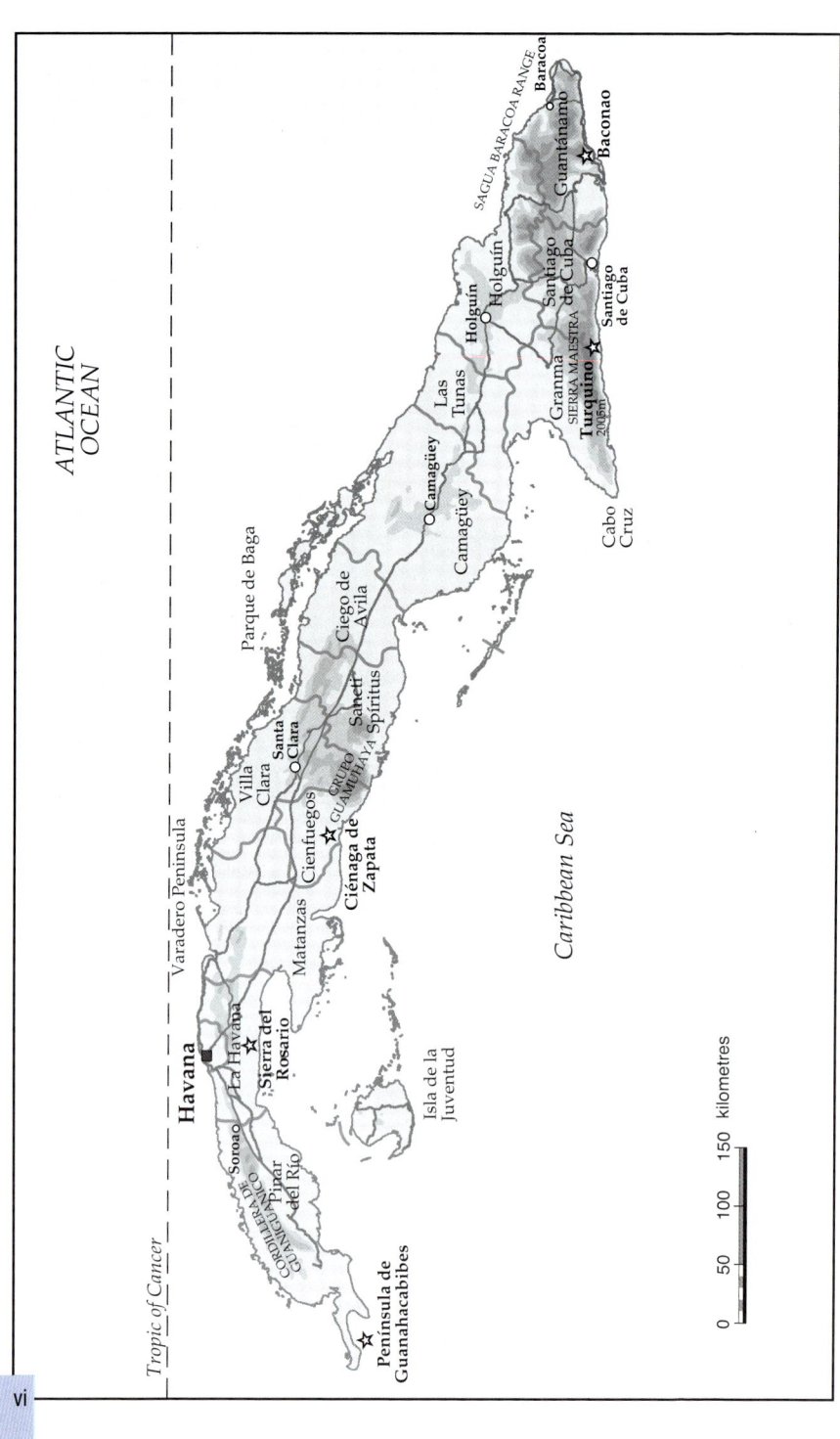

Introduction

This small book has been written not for specialists but for nature-lovers who are visiting Cuba and are interested in identifying the country's flowering herbaceous plants, vines, bushes and trees, whether they be in cities, on the beach, or in the island's woods, savannas or mountains.

The flowering times of the trees are listed as a result of direct observation by the author. The native flora of Cuba is not characterized by large, flamboyant flowers: the fact that Cuba is a small archipelago has caused the endemic flowers to be small (sometimes minuscule), as are their pollinating agents (insects, birds and bats). It is perhaps because of this that, two or three centuries ago, people began to introduce to the country decorative flowering plants that have now become naturalized or are so frequently cultivated that they may now be said to form part of our rich botanical heritage.

In this book the reader will find a hundred flowering plants in order of their common Cuban names. Some 35% of the plants are native to Cuba or naturalized. In each case there is an explanatory text and the book also includes a glossary of botanical terms, although efforts have been made to avoid verbal technicalities. Wherever possible, we have also included other English (Caribbean) names of the species, and both these and the scientific names are included in the indexes.

It was not always easy to capture photographically the precise moment of flowering and we had to closely monitor the progress of each tree, bush and vine to achieve the images you see in this slim volume; this task was made easier by the fact that 86% of the plants featured grow in the National Botanic Garden in Havana. In every case, the reader may compare the reality with the photograph and confirm their identification with the text.

Cuba is an archipelago and is the largest of the Greater Antilles in the West Indies. It is located to the south of the Tropic of Cancer between 74°8' and 84°58' W longitude and between 19°50' and 23°17' N latitude, 180 km (110 miles) south of Florida (USA) and 210 km (130 miles) east of Yucatan (Mexico); to the south, Jamaica is 140 km (87 miles) away and to the east only 77 km (48 miles) of ocean lie between Cuba and Haiti. The main island, Cuba, is long and narrow, extending in direction from the northwest to the southeast. It is 1 250 km (775 miles) long at its longest point and has 5 746 km (3 400 miles) of coastline with hundreds of beautiful beaches. Plains form two-thirds of the island's terrain. It has four principal mountain ranges: the Guaniguanico in the west which includes the smaller ranges of Los Órganos and del Rosario; the Guamuhaya in the centre of the island, with the smaller Escambray range; in the southeast of the island, the large Sierra Maestra range includes the highest mountain in the country, Pico Turquino (1 974 metres or 6 476 feet above sea level) and in the northeast, the Sagua-Baracoa range contains the smaller ranges of Nipe, Cristal, Moa, Toa, Imías and Baracoa.

The Cuban climate is tropical with two seasons: the rainy season from May to October, and the dry season, from November to April. The average annual temperature is 25°C (77°F), with the summer maximum being around 35°C (95°F) in July and an average minimum of 10°C (50°F) in December. Humidity tends to range between 74% and 80% during the day and is often over 90% at night. Annual rainfall depends somewhat on hurricanes and cold fronts; the average figure lies between 1 100 and 1 600 mm (43 and 63 in) per year.

The Caribbean region is one of the most important areas among conservation priorities for the planet. It is considered to be one of the 25 hotspots (areas exhibiting exceptional concentrations of endemic species but facing exceptional loss of habitat) in the world. Cuba, which is the largest territory in the Caribbean, has the region's highest number of endemic plants and has suffered a tremendous destruction of natural habitats during its history, and thus contributes greatly to the consideration of the Caribbean region as an important hotspot.

Cuba has around 7 000 native plants, 51% of which are endemic to the country, which makes it one of the most richly endowed islands in the world. It also has a wide diversity of ecosystems, with eight major types of vegetation. The variety of soil types in the country and the height above sea level greatly contribute to the richness of its flora.

A total of 22% of the territory is under the protected areas system. Six Biosphere Reserves, two World Heritage areas and six Ramsar sites (wetlands) are among the most relevant protected areas.

Abrojo

(Abrojo de la Florida, Bella Hortensia)
Pereskia zinniflora DC.

Synonym: *Rhodocactus cubensis* (Britton & Rose) F.M. Knuth

WARNING: Dangerously prickly.

Family: Cactaceae

Origin: Cuba, endemic.

Plant type: A small, deciduous tree growing up to 4 m (13 ft) high and 25 cm (10 in) in diameter. The trunk and branches are very spiny.

Leaves: Alternate, slightly fleshy, elliptic to obovate, with sharp tips, 1.5–4 cm (½–1½ in) long. Deep brilliant green on both sides, without spines.

Flowers: The showy pink-purple flowers appear singly, with male and female flowers appearing on different trees. They attract so many bees that the trees themselves seem to be buzzing and can be heard from over 3 m (10 ft) away. Blossoms from April to June.

Fruit: A berry of 2–3 cm (¾–1 in) diameter, containing numerous small, black, angular seeds embedded in white pulp.

Comments: Although this tree is beautiful its spines render it unpopular, so it has become scarce and the species requires protection. It is found in the wild in the dry woodlands of the Eastern provinces of Cuba, as well as in damper soil in the centre of the island, where it often grows alongside the *Copernicia* palm.

Adelfa

(Rosa Francesa, Oleander)
Nerium oleander L.

WARNING: This plant is extremely poisonous: its juice contains cyanide.

Family: Apocynaceae

Origin: Europe (Mediterranean region).

Plant type: Leafy shrub, 2–3 m (6½–10 ft) high.

Leaves: Abundant, opposite or in whorls of three; spear-shaped, leathery, 15–20 cm (6–8 in) long, dull green.

Flowers: Very decorative, in terminal clusters of trumpet-shaped pink, pinkish-red or white flowers with five rounded lobes at the outer end of the tube. There is a whorl of short appendages in the throat of the flower.

Fruit: Very rare in Cuba. It is propagated from cuttings.

Comments: In spite of being so poisonous, this plant is very common in gardens and beside roads, especially by the sea. A beautiful cultivar of Adelfa has been developed that has a 'double' corolla of bright pink petals.

Aguinaldo Amarillo

(Yellow Morning Glory)
Merremia umbellata (L.) Hallier f.

Family: Convolvulaceae

Origin: Widespread throughout the Tropics.

Plant type: A vine which climbs to about 5 m (16 ft). It has milky sap.

Leaves: Alternate, heart-shaped with pointed tips, up to 7 cm (2¾ in) long.

Flowers: Grouped in bunches in the axils of the leaves, bell-shaped, bright yellow, about 3 cm (1 in) long, appearing from December to March.

Fruit: The small pod contains dark brown, velvety seeds.

Comment: A native plant common throughout the island; it prefers damp soil. Sometimes it is seen growing with the white-blossomed Aguinaldo Blanco (*Turbina corymbosa*) and pinky-mauve Marrullero (*Ipomoea tiliacea*) in a very attractive colour combination. The flowers of Aguinaldo Amarillo open daily, around late morning.

Aguinaldo Blanco

(Aguinaldo, Aguinaldo de Pascuas, Aguinaldo de Campanilla, Christmas Pops)
Turbina corymbosa (L.) Raf.

Family: Convolvulaceae

Origin: Tropical America.

Plant type: A woody vine which climbs to about 10 m (33 ft) high. The oldest stems of the plant grow up to 3 cm (1 in) diameter.

Leaves: Alternate, heart-shaped with pointed tips, dark green above and lighter below, 3–5 cm (1–2 in) long.

Flowers: Numerous bell-shaped flowers appear in axillary bunches from November and throughout the winter. They are white on the outside, yellow deepening to dark violet on the inside, and are strongly scented.

Fruit: A small pod to which the dry sepals of the flower remain attached; contains one seed.

Comments: The honey produced by bees that visit this plant is clear with an especially delicious and fragrant flavour. Aguinaldo Blanco flowers particularly profusely in late December, hence the common name 'Aguinaldo de Pascuas'.

Ajo De Jardín

Tulbaghia violacea Harv.

WARNING: Poisonous.

Family: Alliaceae

Origin: South Africa.

Plant type: Perennial, 20–30 cm (8–12 in) high, growing in clumps from bulbs.

Leaves: The long, deep green shiny leaves grow directly from the bulb; they measure about 20 cm in length and smell strongly of garlic.

Flowers: 10 to 13 trumpet-shaped flowers appear on a stalk about 40 cm (16 in) long. They have six light violet petals bearing a whorl of three appendages in the flower mouth; a central darker line runs down the whole petal which is about 1–2 cm (½–¾ in) in both length and width. The flowers, which also smell of garlic, appear from April to August.

Fruit: Not commonly seen; asexually reproduced in Cuba.

Comments: This plant is growing in popularity, often being used in the decorative borders of flower beds in Cuban gardens. Although it is related to garlic, it is highly poisonous.

Alamanda

(Flor de Barbero, Buttercup Flower, Yellow Bell)
Allamanda cathartica L.

WARNING: This plant is extremely poisonous.

Family: Apocynaceae

Origin: Brazil.

Plant type: Shrubby vine.

Leaves: In whorls of four, light green, with a waxy surface.

Flowers: Golden-yellow, cup-shaped, with five petals, 10–12 cm (4–5 in) across. It flowers throughout the year but mainly in summer.

Fruit: The plant does not produce fruits in Cuba.

Comments: A fast-growing ornamental plant widely used in all Cuban cities. It is easily reproduced from cuttings. The milky sap of this plant is highly toxic.

Algodón

(Wild Cotton, Cotton)
Gossypium spp.

Family: Malvaceae

Origin: Tropical regions of the world.

Plant type: A shrub of up to 3 m (10 ft) in height.

Leaves: Growing opposite one another, usually lobed with heart-shaped bases, dull green, up to 10 cm (4 in) long. The young shoots are hairy.

Flowers: Appear singly on stalks, with three modified narrower leaves at the base of each flower. The corolla is only partly opened even at maturity, with five pale yellow petals fading to pink, about 4–5 cm (1½–2 in) in length and width.

Fruit: The rough triangular-shaped seed pod splits open when ripe to expose the white cotton fibres, which surround the brown seeds.

Comments: Cotton has been cultivated in the Tropics for centuries. In Cuba there is extensive evidence of the Taino Indians having harvested wild cotton, which they spun and wove into hammocks, ropes and other items for daily use. There are two species of Cotton (*G. hirsutum* and *G. barbadense*) that grow in coastal woodlands in every Cuban province.

Alpinia

(Ginger Lily)
Alpinia purpurata (Vieill.) K. Schum.

Family: Zingiberaceae

Origin: New Guinea and Southeastern Asia.

Plant type: A perennial with leafy shoots about 2 m (6½ ft) high when in flower; its rhizomes are covered with overlapping brown scales.

Leaves: Spear-shaped, up to 70 cm (2 ¼ft) long and 15 cm (6 in) wide, narrower at the tips, the upper surfaces being brilliant green with paler green undersides.

Flowers: In spikes at the end of the stalks; shiny, waxy red bracts spirally disposed, each of which contains a tiny flower. The plant blooms all year round.

Fruit: A black, spherical seed pod containing numerous small seeds.

Comments: Alpinia is a favourite garden plant throughout the Caribbean due to its beautiful red flowers and attractive leaves. It is extensively used for flower arrangements. The pink variety of the plant is less commonly cultivated. A highly ornamental form of the plant with variegated leaves is grown in Cuba.

Anturio

(Corazón De Jesús, Anthurium, Heart Flower, Flamingo Flower)
Anthurium andraeanum Linden ex André

Family: Araceae

Origin: Ecuador to Colombia.

Plant type: Herbaceous plant which grows in clumps.

Leaves: Heart-shaped to ovate with sharp tips, leathery, bright green above and opaque, light green beneath, 15–20 cm (6–8 in) long and 7–12 cm (2¾–5 in) wide.

Flowers: As in all the members of this family, the real flowers are numerous and very small, located in a tube-like yellow or white structure 5–6 cm (2–2¼ in) long called the 'spadix', which is in turn surrounded by a modified leaf called the 'spathe'. This shiny red, white or pink 'flower' constitutes the ornamental part of the plant, which blooms all year round.

Fruit: Small, round, sunken within the spadix; each one contains a seed.

Comments: Anturio is a very useful ornamental plant. It is particularly attractive in floral arrangements because of its long-lasting beauty. It grows and flowers most successfully at altitudes above 300 m (1000 ft).

Asistasia

Asystasia gangetica (L.) T. Anderson

Family: Acanthaceae

Origin: India, Asia; widely cultivated in the Tropics.

Plant type: A herbaceous branching plant, which grows to about 60 cm (2 ft) high or climbs to 3–4 m (10–13 ft).

Leaves: Heart-shaped with very sharp tips, from 3 cm (1 in) to 11 cm (4½ in) long.

Flowers: Single blooms appear on one side of the tips of the branches. The calyx is green with spear-shaped sepals; the corolla is light yellow, trumpet-shaped with five lobes, one of which is larger than the others, causing the flower to appear asymmetrical.

Fruit: A seed pod 2.5 cm (1 in) long, irregular and narrow, which opens into two valves when dry to reveal four seeds.

Comments: Asistacia has delicate light yellow flowers and is widely cultivated in gardens. It is naturalized in other Caribbean islands. Its botanical name is a reference to the River Ganges.

Ave del Paraíso

(Estrelizia, Bird of Paradise Flower)
Strelitzia reginae Aiton

Family: Strelitziaceae

Origin: South Africa.

Plant type: Herbaceous plant, 50–70 cm (20–28 in) high, grows in clumps.

Leaves: Rigid, oval with pointed tips, the central rib being coarse-textured and of a reddish colour, measuring up to 50 cm (20 in) long and 20 cm (8 in) at their widest.

Flowers: A very unusual inflorescence, having a strong stalk longer than the surrounding leaves, which bends at the top and culminates in a pointed sheath from whose interior the flowers protrude, each consisting of three vertical pointed orange-red petals and a blue, waxy, pointed, rigid structure which constitutes the male part of the flower. The whole inflorescence is about 20 cm (8 in) long and appears principally during the summertime.

Fruit: Not seen in Cuba; this plant is reproduced asexually.

Comments: Ave del Paraíso is the most exotic flower in the Caribbean. It was introduced into Cuba in the middle of the twentieth century and is cultivated everywhere but most successfully at altitudes above 300 m (1000 ft). Note also the related species *Strelitzia nicolai*, which has blue and white flowers and grows up to 3 m (10 ft) high.

Bauhinia Roja

Bauhinia galpinii N. E. Brown

Family: Caesalpiniaceae (Leguminosae)

Origin: South Africa.

Plant type: A shrub with spreading, climbing branches.

Leaves: Alternate, double-lobed (as are all the leaves of plants in this genus), leathery, light green, 6–7 cm (about 2½ in) long and 7–10 cm (2¾–4 in) wide.

Flowers: Very showy, in loose clusters of red-orange flowers with five petals, resembling a butterfly. Blossoms in the rainy season (May to October).

Fruit: A bean-shaped, flat, brown seed pod about 8 cm (3 in) long ending in a beak, with flat seeds.

Comments: This beautiful climbing shrub was introduced into Cuba in the first half of the twentieth century by the former Atkins Garden of Harvard University (now the Botanic Garden of Cienfuegos). *Bauhinia Roja* is an excellent ornamental for use in open spaces, well adapted to our climatic conditions.

Bienvestido

(Bien vestida, Amor y Celos, Piñón Florido, Piñón Amoroso, Mata-Ratón, Quick Stick, Pea Tree)
Gliricidia sepium (Jacq.) Kunth ex Walp.

WARNING: Both the roots and the bark are extremely poisonous.

Family: Fabaceae (Leguminosae)

Origin: Tropical America.

Plant type: A small deciduous tree growing up to 10 m (13 ft), although in Cuba it seldom achieves this height.

Leaves: Alternate, compound, with 7 to 17 ovate to spear-shaped leaflets, 3–7 cm (1–3 in) long and 2–3 cm (¾–1 in) wide, with pointed tips, light green; deciduous during the winter (December to March).

Flowers: Appear in axillary clusters about 15 cm (6 in) long of numerous pinkish-mauve to white blossoms, 1.5–2 cm (½–¾ in) wide, with a corolla of five petals. The tree blooms to very decorative effect in March, before its leaves have appeared.

Fruit: Bienvestido produces a bean-like seed pod, 10–15 cm (4–6 in) long and 1.5 cm (½ in) wide, but the tree rarely fruits in Cuba where it is mainly propagated by large cuttings which root rapidly.

Comments: 'Bien vestido' translates into English as 'well-dressed', an appropriate name for a tree which produces a glorious show of flowers, somewhat resembling cherry blossom, but only lasting for a few days. The tree is planted for shade on coffee plantations and is also used to create hedges on cattle farms. The termite-proof wood is often used for furniture and the leaves are fed to cattle. The honey produced by bees that visit Bienvestido trees is especially delicious.

Bija

(Achiote)
Bixa orellana L.

Family: Bixaceae

Origin: Tropical America.

Plant type: Shrub or small tree with yellow sap.

Leaves: Perennial, alternate, ovate to heart-shaped with sharp tips and long petioles; deep green, about 20 cm (8 in) long and 4–15 cm (1½–6 in) wide.

Flowers: Very decorative, in terminal clusters, with five pink overlapping petals, twisted in the bud and having numerous stamens. Flowers from June to November.

Fruit: The brown seed pods are 3–4 cm (1–1½ in) long and wide with rough outer surfaces; they open as two valves revealing numerous red, angular seeds.

Comments: Bija is a pre-Columbian plant which is thought to have been brought to Cuba by the Arawak Indians. They used the orange dye contained in its seeds to paint their bodies for religious ceremonies, and for protection against bites and stings from mosquitoes and other insects. The dye obtained from Bija is still widely used in Cuban traditional cooking to add a 'saffron' tinge to rice and meat. There is a garden variety with bright red seed pods.

Boniato de Playa

(Beach Morning Glory, Goat Foot)
Ipomoea pes-caprae (L.) R. Br. subsp. *brasiliensis* (L.) Ooststr.

Family: Convolvulaceae

Origin: Sandy coastal areas in the Tropics.

Plant type: A creeping herbaceous plant whose stems become woody as they age, up to 10 m (33 ft) long.

Leaves: Alternate, kidney-shaped to round, leathery with long petioles, 6–12 cm (2–5 in) long, and 4–7 cm (1½–8 in) wide, pale green.

Flowers: The large single flower appears in the axil of the leaf, the calyx being yellowish-green with five sepals. The corolla is tubular and 4–5 cm (1½–2 in) long, terminating in five rounded pink-purple lobes. The plant flowers all year round.

Fruit: A spherical seed pod containing four brown, hairy seeds 8 mm (³⁄₁₀ in) long.

Comments: Boniato de Playa is a very common plant on Cuban beaches where it creeps over the surface of the dunes, adding a note of colour and freshness to this hot and arid landscape with its large pinkish-mauve flowers and pale green leaves. The common name 'Boniato de Playa' is referred to the close resemblance to *Ipomoea batatas*, the sweet potato plant.

Bougainvillea

(Flor de Papel, Trinitaria)
Bougainvillea glabra Choisy

WARNING: This plant has extremely sharp spines.

Family: Nyctaginaceae

Origin: Brazil.

Plant type: A woody climber of about 1.5 m (5 ft) high. The branches are cylindrical and can reach 5–6 cm (2–2¼ in) in diameter when they are very old. The plant is covered with sharp spines.

Leaves: Alternate, oval to heart-shaped with a pointed tip, deep green, 5–10 cm (2–4 in) long and 5–8 cm (2–3 in) wide.

Flowers: In very showy groups at the ends of the branches. The real flowers appear in groups of three, each one surrounded by a coloured modified leaf (bract), heart-shaped at the base and 2–4 cm (¾–1½ in) long. These bracts may be red, pink, orange-yellow, white or purple. The small flowers are greenish-white and tubular,

terminating in 8 to 10 lobes 2.5–3 mm (about ⅒ in) long. Bougainvillea blossoms all year round, but principally during the drier winter months.

Fruit: Not seen. Propagated from cuttings.

Comments: A very popular plant in Cuba, especially for the creation of hedges, due to its vigorous growth, spiny branches and the fact that it needs no special care.

Brujita

(Bruja, Rain Flower, Wind Flower)
Zephyranthes spp.

Family: Amaryllidaceae

Origin: Tropical America.

Plant type: Small, bulbous annual, which grows in clumps.

Leaves: Narrow, dark green and glossy, of varying lengths according to the species.

Flowers: Single on long stalks, cup-shaped with six long lobes united at their base; white, yellow, pale or dark pink, with sizes varying according to the species.

Fruit: The dry seed pod with three internal cavities contains numerous flat, black seeds.

Comments: Brujitas include native and cultivated species which sometimes become naturalized. The common name 'Brujita' (little witch) refers to the fact that the plant disappears during the dry season, then suddenly appears from the subterranean bulb and bursts into flower after the first rains. There are five species reported in Cuba, one of which (*Zephyranthes rosea*) is native, but it is also cultivated along with the other four species.

Caliandra Roja

(Caliandra, Mimosa, Red Head Calliandra)
Calliandra haematocephala Hassk.

Family: Mimosaceae (Leguminosae)

Origin: South America.

Plant type: A shrub with dense foliage.

Leaves: Alternate, compound with leaflets disposed in pairs, asymmetrical, bright green above, with distinct veins. The leaflets are 2–5 cm (¾–2 in) long and 1–2 cm (½–¾ in) wide.

Flowers: Very attractive; the main visible structures are the numerous long, red stamens which make the flowers look like powder puffs. Flowers mainly in winter.

Fruit: A long, dry, brown seed pod 8–12 cm (3–5 in) long, containing several flat seeds.

Comments: Caliandra Roja is widely cultivated for its attractive red 'power puff' flowers. A related species, *Calliandra surinamensis*, whose stamens are white or pink, is also often planted in Cuba as an ornamental.

Calistemon

(Palo Basigato, Falso Sauce, Bottle Brush Tree)
Callistemon speciosus (Sims) Sweet

Family: Myrtaceae

Origin: Australia.

Plant type: A medium-sized tree bearing a cascade of weeping branches.

Leaves: Alternate, small, rough-textured, linear to spear-shaped with pointed tips, slightly hairy, light green.

Flowers: Inflorescences at the ends of the branches contain numerous flowers disposed closely one to another around the stem. The flowers have a tiny calyx and corolla with long red stamens and style, each one having the appearance of a diminutive feather-duster, whilst the whole inflorescence looks like a red bottle brush. Blossoms from March to April.

Fruit: A small brown cylindrical seed pod with three or four cavities containing the powder-like seeds that are dispersed by the wind when the fruit is dry.

Comments: This beautiful tree is often used as an ornamental in parks and avenues; it is sometimes confused with a willow because of its weeping branches. Closely related species also used for ornamental purposes are *C. citrinus*, *C. hortensis* and *C. lanceolatus*. Bees frequently visit Calistemon trees, for their flowers are particularly abundant in nectar.

Campana

(Angel´s Tears, Angel's Trumpet)
Brugmansia x candida Pers.

WARNING: This plant is extremely poisonous.

Family: Solanaceae

Origin: Peru; cultivated throughout the Tropics.

Plant type: A shrub which grows to about 2 m (6½ ft) high.

Leaves: Alternate, large, elliptical leaves with round bases and pointed tips, up to 30 cm (1 ft) long.

Flowers: Campana has a pendulous bell-shaped flower with a long green calyx. The corolla has five lobes with a small point at the end of each one. The flower, which can measure up to 30 cm (1 ft) long, is cream-coloured whilst in bud and white when fully open.

Fruit: A spherical capsule; the plant is commonly reproduced from cuttings.

Comments: Despite being poisonous, this plant also has a beneficial use: it contains an alkaloid called daturine, which is obtained from its leaves and flowers and may be used for the relief of asthma and other pulmonary complaints. It is however extremely dangerous to take this drug unless it has been specifically prescribed by a doctor.

Campana Gallega

(Aguinaldo Morado, Potato Bush)
Ipomoea carnea Jacq. subsp. *fistulosa* (Mart. ex Choisy) D. F. Austin

Synonym: *Ipomoea crassicaulis* (Benth.) B. L. Robinson

Family: Convolvulaceae

Origin: Brazil.

Plant type: A perennial shrub, 1–2.5 m (3–8 ft) high.

Leaves: Opposite, heart-shaped, with sharp tips.

Flowers: Bell-shaped, pink to pale purple, slightly furry, measuring 6–8 cm (2¼–3 in). Blooms all year round, copiously during the rainy season.

Fruit: Not seen. This plant is propagated from cuttings.

Comments: Although a native of Brazil, this plant is widely grown in Cuban gardens and parks due to its easy propagation by cuttings and its fast growth, in addition to its beautiful flowers, which appear throughout the year.

Caña Mexicana

(Cañuela Santa, Spiral Flag)
Costus speciosus (Koenig, J.) Sm.

Family: Zingiberaceae

Origin: Southeastern Asia.

Plant type: Herbaceous with a tubular, spirally marked stem. The rhizomes branch and spread to form large colonies.

Leaves: Growing alternately, the sheaths overlapping one another, bright green on the upper surface, densely furry beneath; up to 20 cm (8 in) long and 8–10 cm (3–4 in) wide.

Flowers: Appearing in terminal spikes with overlapping bracts. The calyx is crimson, the corolla is short and tubular at the base, the lobes are broad and thin and pinkish-white in colour, with one of them being broader. The entire flower is about 5 cm (2 in) long and slightly scented.

Fruit: The plant does not fruit; it is asexually propagated by rhizomes.

Comments: Caña Mexicana is a very common plant in domestic gardens. It is naturalized in some countries of Tropical America and the Caribbean, including Cuba where it is renowned for its medicinal properties: an infusion brewed from the rhizomes and the stems acts as a diuretic.

Cañafístola

(Caña Fistula, Shower of Gold, Indian Laburnum)
Cassia fistula L.

Family: Caesalpiniaceae (Leguminosae)

Origin: Tropical Asia.

Plant type: A small deciduous tree, 7–8 m (23–26 ft) high, with a straight, brown trunk and an oval canopy.

Leaves: Alternate, compound, very large, up to 50 cm (20 in) long, with four to eight pairs of leaflets 10–12 cm (4–5 in) long, bright green above and silvery below.

Flowers: Very showy, in large, cascading racemes, 30–50 cm (12–20 in) long, each containing up to 30 golden-yellow flowers of five petals suspended from a small stalk. The plant flowers from May to August.

Fruit: The long, pendant, cylindrical brown pod about 40 cm (16 in) long and 2–3 cm (¾–1 in) in diameter contains numerous flat seeds surrounded by a sweet brown pulp; they take over a year to ripen.

Comments: Cañafístola is one of our most beautiful exotic flowering trees and is used extensively throughout the island of Cuba in streets and parks. The pulp in the seedpods is used as a laxative; Cañafístola was one of the earliest medicinal plants to be introduced into the island.

Cañandonga

(Cañafístula Cimarrona, Coral Shower, Horse Cassia)
Cassia grandis L.f.

Family: Caesalpiniaceae (Leguminosae)

Origin: Eastern Cuba; Central and South America.

Plant type: A deciduous tree with a straight, grey trunk, growing to 15–30 m (50–80 ft) high.

Leaves: Alternate, compound with 8 to 20 pairs of leaflets, 5 cm (2 in) long and 10–15 cm (4–6 in) wide; deep green.

Flowers: Highly decorative; the coral-coloured flowers have six rounded petals 15 mm (½ in) wide, with long, golden-yellow stamens, in dense axillary clusters, 10–20 cm (4–8 in) long. Flowers briefly and spectacularly at the start of the rainy season (May to June).

Fruit: Cylindrical, brown, rough-textured seed pods about 30–90 cm (1–3 ft) long which contain numerous flat seeds disposed like piles of coins in individual cells, embedded in an evil-smelling (but delicious-tasting) brown pulp.

Comments: Cañandonga is very common in the Eastern provinces of Cuba. It is found in semi-deciduous forests and is cultivated in parks and gardens where it is prized for its spectacular blossom. The pulp of the fruit is often made into drinks and is also used medicinally for its laxative properties and for increasing the haemoglobin level in the blood.

Cardenal

(Arbol Cardenal, Pride of Guatemala)
Phyllocarpus septentrionalis Donn. Smith

Family: Caesalpiniaceae (Leguminosae)

Origin: Guatemala and Honduras.

Plant type: A tall deciduous tree with arching branches, up to 20 m (8 in) high.

Leaves: Alternate, compound of leaflets about 8 cm (3 in) long and 5 cm (2 in) wide, disposed in four to eight pairs, bright green.

Flowers: Grouped in dense clusters of tiny scarlet-red flowers of six petals with long, red stamens. Flowers during the dry season (February to March).

Fruit: The flat seed pods, about 15 cm (6 in) long and 5 cm (2 in) wide, burst open to allow the dispersal of the winged seeds.

Comments: Although it is not very common, Cardenal is one of Cuba's most spectacular trees. A particularly beautiful clump of Cardenal trees may be seen in the Central America zone of the Cuban National Botanic Garden in Havana.

Carolina

(Shaving Brush Tree)
Pseudobombax ellipticum (Kunth) Dugand

Synonym: *Bombax ellipticum* Kunth

Family: Malvaceae (formerly Bombacaceae)

Origin: Mexico, Central America.

Plant type: A tree that grows up to 10 m (33 ft). The main trunk is cylindrical, green to greyish-green, with branches extending from its lower parts, and becomes extremely wide when the tree is old, apart from when it is propagated asexually from the branches. The canopy is spreading, the direction of branch growth inclining towards the horizontal.

Leaves: A finger-like, partially folded compound of five to six leaflets measuring 5–30 cm (2–12 in) long and 4–17 cm (1½–7 in) wide, distributed at the end of the branches; vivid green. New leaves are bright red, forming a spectacular contrast with the green trunk.

Flowers: Appearing in pairs or singly at the end of the branches, they look like shaving brushes, having numerous long, brilliant pink or white stamens. The corolla has five dark or light pink petals, which curl when the flower is open. The flower, which is approximately 15 cm (6 in) long, appears from February to April during the dry season when the tree is without leaves.

Fruit: Not commonly produced by Carolina trees growing in Cuba, probably due to the lack of a pollinating insect.

Comments: A spectacular tree, from which the flowers fall to form a pink or white carpet. Commonly used in landscape gardening for the beauty of its trunk, leaves and flowers and its tolerance of poorly irrigated soil.

Casia Nodosa

(Casia de Java, Apple Blossom Cassia, Nodding Cassia)
Cassia javanica L.

Synonym: *Cassia nodosa* Buch.-Ham. ex Roxb.

Family: Caesalpiniaceae (Leguminosae)

Origin: Southeastern Asia.

Plant type: A deciduous tree with a straight trunk and numerous knotted branches and light brown bark. The canopy is spreading, with dense foliage. It can grow to about 30 m (100 ft), but is much shorter in Cuba.

Leaves: Alternate, compound, with numerous dark green leaflets.

Flowers: Highly decorative, appearing in dense clusters; the flowers are pink fading to near-white, which gives them a variegated appearance. Each flower has five petals with long curved stamens and a subtle scent of apples. Blooms from April to June, before the new leaves appear.

Fruit: A long, cylindrical, brown seed pod 20–30 cm (8–12 in) long, with numerous flat seeds stacked up like piles of small coins.

Comments: This is a highly decorative tree, widely cultivated in tropical countries. It was introduced into Cuba during the first half of the twentieth century and is now grown in numerous public spaces. An outstanding group may be seen in the Japanese Garden of the National Botanic Garden in Havana, where it was planted instead of the Cherry, which would not have survived in the tropical heat. Its delicious scent and decorative flowers are a worthy addition to the garden.

Clerodendro

(Clerodendro rojo)
Clerodendron x speciosum Dombrain

Family: Lamiaceae

Origin: Tropical Africa

Plant type: A leafy, branching climber.

Leaves: Opposite one another, oval with sharp tips, deep green above and paler below, with prominent veins, 7.5–15.5 cm (3–6 in) long and 5–7 cm (2–2¾ in) wide.

Flowers: Very decorative, appearing in axillary clusters. The reddish-purple calyx covers the base of the orange-red corolla, the tube of the corolla is very narrow and its five lobes are rounded, with four pink to red stamens protruding to twice its length. The plant blossoms in the dry season (February to April).

Fruit: Not seen; asexually propagated by cuttings.

Comments: This species is a natural hybrid between *C. thompsoniae* and *C. splendens*. Clerodendro is a beautiful climber, used in gardens to cover walls and fences.

Cola de Camarón

(Cola de Camarón Amarilla, Yellow Shrimp Plant, Golden Candles)
Pachystachys lutea Nees

Family: Acanthaceae

Origin: Tropical America.

Plant type: A shrub growing to about 50 cm (20 in) high.

Leaves: Long, spear-shaped or elliptical with a pointed tip, growing opposite one another or in whorls; dull green, up to 15 cm (6 in) long and 3 cm (1 in) wide.

Flowers: In erect spikes at the ends of stems; the white flowers are encased in yellow bracts. The flowers are tubular, asymmetrical, 3–4 cm (1–1½ in) long. The plant blooms all year round.

Fruit: Not seen. In Cuba this plant is easily propagated from cuttings.

Comments: This evergreen shrub flowers continuously and the same flower can last several weeks if it is not cut. It is for this reason that it is widely cultivated in gardens and public spaces. Another plant of the same family is similarly popular: *Beloperone gutata* is also known as 'Cola de Camarón' (Shrimp Plant), having reddish-brown bracts which look like shrimps' tails.

Colonia

(Boca de Dragón, Cojate, Ginger)
Alpinia zerumbet (Pers.) Burret & R.M.Sm.

Synonym: *Alpinia speciosa* (Wendl.) K. Schum.

Family: Zingiberaceae

Origin: East Asia.

Plant type: A perennial with leafy arching stalks, growing in clumps from rhizomes.

Leaves: Long, spear-shaped with sharp tips, with a brilliant green leathery surface, about 80 cm (32 in) long. The leaf edges are minutely serrated.

Flowers: Showy, in terminal racemes with the stalk bent at right angles to the leaf plane. The flowers are bell-like, white and waxy outside with red and yellow interiors, the corolla having pink patches on the petals, one of which is especially broad. The strongly scented flowers,

which appear mainly during the rainy season, are about 3–4 cm (1–1½ in) wide.

Fruit: A round seed pod containing numerous seeds.

Comments: Colonia is an ornamental and medicinal plant. The beautiful flowers have a scent reminiscent of Eau de Cologne; hence its common name. The rhizome, chopped and steeped in alcohol, is used in massages for the relief of muscular and arthritic pain.

Coral Vegetal

(Gout plant)
Jatropha podagrica Hook.

WARNING: The seeds and sap of this plant are extremely poisonous.

Family: Euphorbiaceae

Plant type: Grotesquely shaped, deciduous, succulent shrub, greatly enlarged at the base and narrowing towards the top, up to 50 cm (20 in) high, containing milky sap.

Leaves: Between 8 cm (3 in) and 20 cm (8 in) wide, rounded with three to five lobes, the long petiole being inserted into the centre of the leaf blade; light green on the upper side, paler beneath.

Flowers: Groups of flowers appear on a long stalk; their colour and shape are similar to those of coral. These small red blooms have five rounded petals and differ slightly in design according to their sex. The plant blooms all year round.

Fruit: A rounded seed pod about 15 mm (½ in) long with three cavities containing one seed each.

Comments: Coral vegetal is a popular plant in rockery gardens to which its unusual appearance gives a distinctive touch.

Coralillo

(Coralilo Rosado, Coral Vine, Mexican Creeper)
Antigonon leptopus Hook. & Arn.

Family: Polygonaceae

Origin: Mexico; grows in all Caribbean countries.

Plant type: A vine around 10 m (33 ft) long, which climbs using coiled or hooked tendrils.

Leaves: Broadly ovate with curved bases and sharp tips. The veins are very prominent on the underside of the leaf. Up to 13 cm (5 in) long and wide at their broadest part.

Flowers: Very showy, appearing in numerous bunches at the leaf axils and at the ends of the branches, each bunch being about 15–20 cm long. The calyx and the corolla are pink, and both sepals and petals are heart-shaped. Flowers from June to February.

Fruit: Hard, black and angular, surrounded by parts of the flower that remain attached to the fruit. The seed is also fused with the fruit.

Comments: Coralillo is a very common vine in fields and towns in the interior of the country. It is most frequently seen on fences and in hedges. Although it originated in Mexico, it has become naturalized in almost all the Caribbean countries. Coralillo flowers are often visited by bees searching for nectar.

Corona de Cristo

(Gracia de Dios, Crown-of-Thorns)
Euphorbia milii Des Moul.

WARNING: The plant contains a highly poisonous milky sap, which is especially dangerous if it comes into contact with the eyes.

Family: Euphorbiaceae

Origin: Madagascar.

Plant type: A prickly shrub with long thorns, up to 50 cm (20 in) high.

Leaves: Spear-shaped, 5–10 cm (2–4 in) long, growing from thorny, succulent stems.

Flowers: Appear on slender flower stalks, grouped in small clusters of red, pink or yellow bracts with tiny male and female flowers at their centres.

Fruit: Not seen; the plant is easily propagated asexually.

Comments: Corona de Cristo is commonly used in rockery gardens and as a hedging plant.

Cosmos

Cosmos spp.

Family: Asteraceae (Compositae)

Origin: Tropical America.

Plant type: A herb growing to about 60 cm (2 ft) tall.

Leaves: Opposite, deeply divided at the edges, light green in colour and furry on both surfaces. The size depends upon the species.

Flowers: The large flower heads, 3.5–5.5 cm (1¼–2 in) wide, grow on stalks of about 30 cm (1 ft) long. The outer petals are orange-yellow, pink or purple, measuring 2–2.5 cm (¾–1 in) long and serrated at the tips; they surround the densely massed, tiny central flowers.

Fruit: Small black nuts, 1–2 cm (½–¾ in) long.

Comments: Cosmos is widely cultivated in domestic gardens all over the island. Although native to tropical America it is now also common in tropical Asiatic countries. Cosmos sometimes escapes from cultivation. In Cuba, three species are reported: *C. bipinnatus*, *C. caudatus* and *C. sulphureus*, the latter, with orange-yellow flowers, being the most common.

Embeleso

(Azulejo, Jazmín Azul, South African Leadwort)
Plumbago capensis Thunb.

Family: Plumbaginaceae

Origin: South Africa.

Plant type: A small, profusely branching shrub about 50 cm (20 in) high.

Leaves: Alternate, spatula-shaped to oval, bright green, about 10 cm (4 in) long.

Flowers: Trumpet-shaped in spikes at the ends of the branches, slightly hairy, with a sticky calyx. The tube of the corolla is very thin, terminating in five lobes rounded at the tips with a central line running down the whole petal; the flower is light blue and about 5 cm (2 in) long. Flowers all year round.

Fruit: Not seen; the plant is asexually propagated in Cuba.

Comments: Embeleso is cultivated in domestic gardens as a border plant. The light blue colour of its flower is unique amongst ornamental plants in Cuba.

Espino

(Bayoneta, Spanish Bayonet, Spanish Dagger, Yucca)
Yucca aloifolia L.

WARNING: The leaves have very sharp tips.

Family: Agavaceae

Origin: Mexico, southern USA.

Plant type: An arborescent plant with a woody stem, which grows both singly and branched.

Leaves: The leaves are thick, deep green, shaped like a bayonet, ending in a very sharp tip, measuring about 50 cm (20 in) long and 5 cm (2 in) wide. They cover almost the entire length of the central stem and branches.

Flowers: Very decorative terminal conical clusters formed of numerous creamy-white pendant cup-shaped flowers with thick petals, up to 5 cm (2 in) long. Espino flowers from April to September.

Fruit: A cylindrical seed pod, brown to black, about 5 cm (2 in) long, containing many small seeds.

Comments: Espino is a popular garden plant. It is easily propagated from cuttings, it thrives in dry soil with minimal care and has beautiful foliage and flowers. The latter are often eaten, either raw in salads or fried.

Farolito Chino

(Marpacífico chino, Japanese Hibiscus, Coral Hibiscus)
Hibiscus schizopetalus (Mart.) Hook. f.

Family: Malvaceae

Origin: Tropical Africa.

Plant type: A bushy shrub up to 1.5 m (5 ft) high.

Leaves: Alternate, ovate with heart-shaped bases, sharp tips and serrated edges; light green, about 10 cm (4 in) long.

Flowers: The single flowers are suspended on long stalks. Their divided, lacy petals are red or pink; their stamens and style are united in a long, red tubular structure that protrudes beyond the petals. Blossoms all year round, mainly during the rainy season.

Fruit: Not seen; the plant is propagated by cuttings.

Comments: Farolito Chino is a beautiful shrub used as an ornamental plant in gardens, but it is not as abundant as the related Hibiscus (*H. rosa-sinensis*). The pink form is not cultivated in Cuba.

Fausto

(Tumbergia Azul, Tunbergia, Flor de Cera, Blue Trumpet Vine, Clock Vine)
Thunbergia grandiflora Roxb.

Family: Acanthaceae

Origin: India; cultivated in warm regions of the world.

Plant type: A robust woody climber with a hollow stalk, which grows 10–15 m (33–50 ft) high.

Leaves: Opposite, irregularly shaped, broad, ovate with an inverted heart shape at the base from which the principal veins arise, the edges slightly serrated, dark green above and lighter with prominent veins below. Up to 25 cm (10 in) long and 30 cm (12 in) wide.

Flowers: Very large and decorative, grouped in terminal or in axillary bunches, cup-shaped with five lilac-coloured lobes and a splash of yellow at their centre, 6–7 cm (2¼–2¾ in) wide. Blossoms all year round, copiously in February to May.

Fruit: Not known in Cuba; propagated asexually by cuttings.

Comments: This vine is a favourite throughout the island of Cuba due to its ornamental flowers. There is also a variety with white flowers known as 'Fausto Blanco', which is often planted alongside its mauve-coloured counterpart.

Fernandina

(Viuda, Ambarina, Escobilla Morisca, Escabiosa)
Angelonia pilosella J. Kickx

Family: Scrophulariaceae

Origin: Tropical America.

Plant type: Erect, branching perennial herb, growing up to about 40 cm (16 in) high.

Leaves: Opposite, spear-shaped, 3–6 cm (1–2 in) long with finely serrated edges.

Flowers: In erect terminal inflorescences, 6–12 cm (2¼–5 in) long; the tiny, cup-shaped blue-violet flowers terminate in five extended lobes and measure about 15 mm (½ in) across. Blossoms all year round.

Fruit: The small spherical seed pod contains numerous tiny seeds.

Comments: Fernandina is a native plant of the swampy savannas of Central and Western Cuba and is cultivated for its beautiful, delicate flowers. There are two other species of the same genus found on the island, also known as 'Fernandina'.

Flor de la Luna

(Flor de la 'Y', Claro de Luna, Moon Flower, Night Ipomoea)
Ipomoea alba L.

Family: Convolvulaceae

Origin: Tropical Continental America.

Plant type: A climbing plant growing to about 5 m (16 ft), containing milky sap.

Leaves: Alternate, thin, heart-shaped with sharply pointed tips and undulating edges; deep green, up to 15 cm (6 in) in length and width.

Flowers: Growing singly or in small axillary groups, tubular, terminating in a flat, broad, pure white and almost perfectly round corolla with five lobes. The tubular part of the flower is 10–12 cm (4–5 in) long and the disc-like corolla is 9–12 cm (3½–5 in) in diameter. The flowers open at night and remain open until the early hours of the morning, by which time the edges of their petals become somewhat ragged, since they are delicate and very easily damaged by gusts of wind.

Fruit: A small ovoid seed pod 2–3 cm (¾–1 in) long, containing four brown to black seeds about 1 cm (½ in) long.

Comments: Flor de la Luna is widely cultivated and naturalized throughout the Tropics. It is frequently seen climbing on fences, in woodlands and along river banks. The names 'Moon Flower', 'Claro de Luna' and 'Flor de la Luna' refer to the nocturnal opening of its moon-like flowers.

Flor de Muerto

(Clavelón, Copetuda, Marigold)
Tagetes erecta L.

Family: Asteraceae (Compositae)

Origin: Mexico.

Plant type: Annual herbaceous plant.

Leaves: Opposite, serrated at the edges, variable in shape and size, light green.

Flowers: Solitary flower heads, 2.5–7.0 cm (1–2¾ in) wide, upon stalks of 4–15 cm (1½–6 in) long, which are wide below the flower heads, tapering to a more slender stem. The flowers are pale sulphurous yellow to deep orange, and both flowers and leaves have a strong, disagreeable odour. Blooms all year round.

Fruit: Small, nut-like seeds, 7–8 mm (about ¼ in) wide.

Comments: Flor de Muerto takes its name from the fact that is commonly planted in cemeteries. In Mexico, its country of origin, it forms one of the principal visual leitmotifs in the decoration of altars and graves for the celebrations for the Day of the Dead on 2nd November. In Cuba, where the plant has spread from parks and gardens to the wild, several varieties are known, all of which differ in the colour and size of their flowers.

Flor de Nieve

(Jazmín del Vedado, Susana Blanca, White Nightshade)
Thunbergia fragrans Roxb.

Family: Acanthaceae

Origin: Tropical Asia; now widespread.

Plant type: A slender vine growing to about 2 m (6½ ft) high.

Leaves: Growing opposite one another, slightly furry on both surfaces, oval to spear-shaped with irregular edges and pointed tips, deep brilliant green on top and a paler green beneath with prominent veins. They measure 6–12 cm (2¼–5 in) long and 5 cm (2 in) wide.

Flowers: The flowers appear in the axils of leaves, singly or in pairs, with modified leaves covering the calyx. The corolla is tubular, its yellow interior terminating in five white lobes. The flower measures 4–5 cm (1½–2 in) in diameter. Blooms all year round.

Fruit: A capsule 1–2 cm (½–¾ in) long ending in a small point, contains four round seeds.

Comments: This beautiful naturalized plant is commonly found beside roads and at the edges of woods all over the country. It also grows on other Caribbean islands.

Flor de Pascua

(Poinsettia)
Euphorbia pulcherrima Willd. ex Klotzch

WARNING: The plant is extremely poisonous.

Family: Euphorbiaceae

Origin: Mexico.

Plant type: A branching shrub, 2–3 m (6½–10 ft) high.

Leaves: Thin, lobed leaves with long petioles, dull green, up to 20 cm (8 in) long.

Flowers: Appearing at the ends of the branches, the inflorescences consist of bright red pointed bracts (modified leaves) surrounding small yellow flowers which have no corollas. The shrub blossoms from November to January, principally in December; hence the common name 'Flor de Pascua' ('pascua' means Christmas in Spanish).

Fruit: A small pod divided into three cavities, each of which contains a seed. It is, however, unusual to see the fruit of Flor de Pascua in Cuba, where is it normally propagated from cuttings.

Comments: Flor de Pascua is a beautiful flowering winter plant which may be seen all over the world; in temperate countries it is cultivated in pots. Two varieties less commonly seen are the type with yellow bracts and the dramatic 'double' red Flor de Pascua.

Framboyán

(Flamboyán, Flamboyant, Royal Poinciana, Poinciana, Flame Tree)
Delonix regia (Bojer ex Hook.) Raf.

Family: Caesalpiniaceae (Leguminosae)

Origin: Madagascar.

Plant type: A tree that grows up to 20 m (65 ft), usually less in Cuba. Trunk branches from 2 m (6½ ft) above the base with tabular roots up to 90 cm (36 cm) in diameter; smooth, light brown bark. Canopy is widely spreading; occasionally with weeping branches.

Leaves: Alternate, compound of numerous small leaflets 0.4–1 cm (¼–½ in) long, the whole leaf being 30–50 cm (12–20 in) long; light green. The leaves fall during the dry season.

Flowers: Very large and decorative, in numerous large axillary and terminal clusters of seven or more red-orange flowers covering the tree; the flowers have five petals, one of which is white with red spots. Blossoms from June to August, after which the new leaves appear.

Fruit: The large, pendulous, dark brown, flat, woody seed pod opens into two parts when dry, to release the seeds.

Comments: Framboyán is one of most decorative ornamental trees to be found in the Tropics and from early June the city of Havana glows with Framboyan flowers. The tree is planted in the countryside beside roads as well as in parks and avenues. The seed pods are used for handcrafts. Its common name is derived from the French flamboyant.

Framboyán Amarillo

(Yellow Flamboyant)
Peltophorum pterocarpum (DG.) K. Heyne

Synonym: *Peltophorum ferrugineum* Benth.

Family: Caesalpiniaceae (Leguminosae)

Origin: Tropical Asia and Australia.

Plant type: A tree which grows up to 24 m (80 ft) high, usually less in Cuba, with a straight trunk, up to 80 cm (32 in) in diameter, rough brown bark and a dense, rounded canopy. Perennial.

Leaves: Alternate, compound, feathery, with many small leaflets of 2–2.5 cm (¾–1 in) long and 1 cm (½ in) wide; bright green; the new leaves and buds are coppery-red and have a velvety appearance; the entire leaf is about 50 cm (20 in) long.

Flowers: Showy, in erect racemes of 20 to 30 flowers at the ends of the branches and twigs, bright yellow, with five petals and a brown, furry stripe where they meet at the centre of the flower, frilly edges, 2–3 cm (¾–1 in) across. Lightly scented. Blossoms all year round but mainly in the rainy season.

Fruit: The flat seeds are contained within a flat, coppery-red or brown seed pod measuring about 10 cm by 2.5 cm (4 in by 1 in).

Comments: This ornamental tree was introduced into the island during the early part of the twentieth century by the Agronomic Station of Santiago de Las Vegas near Havana. It is a nectar-producing tree often visited by bees.

Frijolillo

(Cucharillo, Guamá Piñón, Juravaina)
Hebestigma cubense (Kunth) Urb.

Family: Fabaceae (Leguminosae)

Origin: Cuba, endemic.

Plant type: A small deciduous tree, 5–12 m (16–40 ft) high.

Leaves: Alternate, compound, with 7–9 ovate to lance-shaped convex leaflets; 5–15 cm (2–6 in) long, with pointed tips, deep green above and paler beneath.

Flowers: In axillary clusters, 8–15 cm (3–6 in) long; the flower has a light pink corolla of five petals of up to 2 cm (¾ in) long. Blossoms in early spring (March), when the tree is almost bare of leaves; leaf growth overlaps with the end of the flowering period.

Fruit: A black seed pod 10–18 cm (4–7 in) long and 2–3 cm (¾–1 in) wide, with black seeds.

Comments: Frijolillo is an excellent timber tree, having hard dark wood. The tree owes its common name ('frijolillo' means 'little bean') to its seed pods, which look like beans. It grows extensively in dry woods.

Galán de Día

(Jazmín de Día, Wild Jasmine)
Cestrum diurnum L.

WARNING: Poisonous.

Family: Solanaceae

Origin: West Indies.

Plant type: A branching shrub growing to 2 m (6½ft) high.

Leaves: Alternate, oval with sharp tips, leathery, light green with a prominent yellow central vein, pale green beneath, up to 10 cm (4 in) long.

Flowers: In axillary clusters, tubular, terminating in five rounded white lobes 2.5 cm (1 in) long and 3 mm (¹⁄₁₀ in) wide, folded backwards at the tips. Strongly scented. Flowers all year round.

Fruit: A rounded, fleshy, purplish-black berry about 6 mm (¼ in) in diameter, containing four to five seeds.

Comments: Galán de Día is a native shrub cultivated in domestic gardens; it also grows beside roads and in woods all over the island.

Galán de Noche

(Galán, Nabasco, Flor de Clavo)
Brunfelsia nitida Benth.

Family: Solanaceae

Origin: Cuba, endemic.

Plant type: A small shrub with few branches and leaves.

Leaves: Alternate, oval, narrow at the base with very sharp tips, bright green on the upper side and paler below, 4–10 cm (1½–4 in) long and 1.5–4 cm (½–1½ in) wide.

Flowers: Appearing singly in the axils of leaves, trumpet-shaped with a very long, straight tube terminating in five rounded creamy-white lobes. Very strongly scented at night; hence the common name 'Galán de Noche' (Gallant of the Night). Blossoms from May to August.

Fruit: The orange, rounded seed pods about 2 cm (¾ in) in diameter contain several seeds.

Comments: Galán de Noche is one of few endemic plants cultivated in Cuban domestic gardens. Its natural habitat is alluvial soil near rivers and streams.

Galán Morado

(Lila de las Antillas)
Brunfelsia cestroides A. Rich.

Family: Solanaceae

Origin: Cuba, endemic.

Plant type: A shrub with slender stems, about 1 m (3 ft) high.

Leaves: Alternate, elliptical, narrowed towards the petiole, 2–5 cm (¾–2 in) long and 0.5–2 cm (¼–¾ in) wide; light green.

Flowers: The single flower appears in the leaf axil. The small, bell-shaped calyx has five teeth; the corolla is tubular and slightly curved, 2 cm (¾ in) long, terminating in rounded lobes. The flower is lilac-coloured, gradually turning to white as the flower fades. The plant blossoms several times a year.

Fruit: A spherical, orange, fleshy seed pod measuring about 5 mm (¼ in) in diameter, to which the calyx of the flower continues to adhere throughout the ripening of the fruit.

Comments: Galán Morado is a graceful little shrub, endemic to Cuba, which might usefully be introduced to cultivation so that its masses of small lilac flowers and yellow fruits could be used for ornamental purposes. It grows widely in brush throughout the island.

Garbancillo

(Violetina, No-Me-Olvides, Júpiter Cimarrón, Fruta de Iguana, Golden Dewdrop, Pigeon Berry, Sky Flower)
Duranta erecta L

Synonym: *Duranta repens* L.

WARNING: This plant is poisonous.

Family: Verbenaceae

Origin: Tropical America.

Plant type: A leafy shrub or small tree growing up to 6 m (20 ft) high, with slender, pendent branches which occasionally bear spines.

Leaves: Growing opposite one another, the bright green leaves are ovate to elliptical with serrated edges but vary widely in shape and size.

Flowers: In loose axillary or terminal clusters of small lilac, violet, blue or white flowers, tubular, terminating in five rounded lobes measuring about 1 cm (½ in) across. Flowers all year round but mainly from April to September.

Fruit: The small hard yellow fruit, which looks like a chick pea and has a little beak at the top, contains four seeds.

Comments: Garbancillo is a commonly cultivated shrub throughout Cuba and the Caribbean due to its attractive flowers and fruits. The fruit is consumed by birds but can be toxic to children.

Gardenia

(Jazmín del Cabo, Cape Jessamine)
Gardenia jasminoides J. Ellis

Family: Rubiaceae

Origin: South Africa.

Plant type: A leafy shrub about 1.5 m (5 ft) high.

Leaves: Opposite, leathery, elliptical with sharp tips, brilliant green above and paler below, 5–10 cm (2–4 in) long.

Flowers: Large decorative single white flowers with numerous petals in a rose-like disposition, 8–10 cm (3–4 in) across. Strongly scented. Blossoms May to June.

Fruit: Not seen; propagated asexually.

Comments: Gardenia is an evergreen shrub often cultivated in domestic gardens for its perfumed white flowers and glossy leaves.

Granito de Oro

(Botón de Oro)
Galphimia glauca Cav.

Synonym: *Thryallis glauca* (Cav.) Kuntze

Family: Malpighiaceae

Origin: Mexico and Central America.

Plant type: A branching shrub with slender stems, growing up to 1.5 m (5 ft) high. The young twigs are covered with fine red hairs.

Leaves: Opposite, ovate to oval, with sharp pointed tips, brilliant green above and paler beneath, 1–5 cm (½–2 in) long.

Flowers: In profusely branching clusters, the tiny flowers are 7–12 mm (¼–½ in) long and have five yellow petals, which narrow abruptly at the base. Blossoms all year round.

Fruit: The tiny triple-lobed seed pods of less than 5 mm (¼ in) long contain one black seed each.

Comments: An ornamental shrub seen in many small gardens, also used to form dense clumps in open garden areas. Granito de Oro grows in the wild in Cuba and is naturalized throughout the Antilles.

Guacamaya

(Peacock Flower, Pride of Barbados)
Caesalpinia pulcherrima (L.) Sw.

WARNING: The stems and twigs bear sharp spines.

Family: Caesalpiniaceae (Leguminosae)

Origin: Uncertain, but probably a native of South America.

Plant type: A shrub or small tree with prickly branches.

Leaves: Alternate, compound, ferny, with many delicate leaflets, 9–18 mm long and 8 mm (¼ in) wide, light green.

Flowers: Appear in racemes at the ends of the branches, with about 20 flowers opening consecutively; butterfly-shaped, with five light orange sepals, one being larger and more concave than the rest; the flower has five orange-red petals with frilly edges of bright yellow shading to red; the stamens and the style are red and extend beyond the corolla; the whole bloom is 2–3 cm (¾–1 in) long. This plant may also be found with completely yellow flowers. Both red and yellow varieties blossom all year round.

Fruit: Flat, thin, bean-like seed pods 8–11 cm (3–4½ in) long and 1.5–2 cm (½–¾ in) wide, which terminate in a point. The seeds are also flat.

Comments: This beautiful shrub is widespread throughout the Caribbean and Central America where it is used as an ornamental plant.

Guacamaya Francesa

(Guacamayón, Hierba de los Herpes, Candlestick, King-of-the-Forest, Ringworm Shrub)
Senna alata (L.) Roxb.

Synonym: *Cassia alata* L.

Family: Caesalpiniaceae (Leguminosae)

Origin: Tropical America.

Plant type: Deciduous, short-lived shrub, 3–5 m (10–16 ft) high.

Leaves: Alternate, compound, very large, with many leaflets 15–20 cm (6–8 in) long and 7–13 cm (2¾–5 in) wide, light green.

Flowers: Very decorative, in axillary racemes 15–20 cm (6–8 in) long which curve upwards from the plane of the leaf. The golden-yellow waxy petals are about 2 cm (¾ in) long. Blossoms in the dry season, after the leaf fall in January–March.

Fruit: The brown, dry, cross-shaped pod 10–15 cm (4–6 in) long contains numerous seeds.

Comments: Guacamaya Francesa is a beautiful garden plant also cultivated for its medicinal properties: the leaves boiled in water are a powerful remedy against herpes of the skin. The plant is naturalized, being found in the wild in swampy soil.

Guayaba

(Guayabo, Guava)
Psidium guajava L.

Family: Myrtaceae

Origin: Tropical America.

Plant type: A small tree, up to 5–6 m (16–20 ft) in height, with a rounded leafy canopy. Slender, profusely branched trunk, with a smooth light brown bark.

Leaves: Opposite, elliptical, the tips may be sharp or blunt; the leaves are dull green on the upper surface, with prominent veins, and measure 7–14 cm (2¾–5½ in) long.

Flowers: Appearing singly or doubly in the leaf axils. The flower has four or five white petals 1.5–2 cm (½–¾ in) wide, with numerous white and yellow stamens appearing at their centre; they look rather like brushes. Flowers sporadically throughout the year, usually during the wetter months.

Fruit: A large, rounded fruit 3–6 cm (1–2¼) in diameter, which turns from green to yellow when ripe; the edible flesh is pink or pale yellow and contains numerous small, hard seeds around its centre.

Comments: Guayaba is a very popular fruit tree in Cuba, having been naturalized in pre-Columbian times when the Indians brought it to the island from the South American continent. It occurs naturally in fields and woods and is also cultivated in domestic gardens and on large fruit farms. Guayaba fruit can be eaten raw and in drinks or cooked in jellies and desserts. The wood is compact and resistant and is used in the countryside for building and cabinet-making. The bark and leaves contain tannins; they are used by practitioners of traditional medicine to heal wounds, and to cure diarrhoea and stomach pain. The fruit is very rich in Vitamin C. A related native species, the fruit of which is highly aromatic, is renowned for its use in the preparation of 'Guayabita del Pinar', a rum-based liquor during whose manufacture small fruits are inserted into the bottles.

Ixora

(Ixora roja, Santa Rita, Flame of the Forest)
Ixora coccinea L.

Family: Rubiaceae

Origin: East Indies (India, China).

Plant type: Shrub growing to 3 m (10 ft) high.

Leaves: Opposite, leathery, ovate to elliptical, dark green, shiny, about 10 cm (4 in) long.

Flowers: The luxuriant show of flowers appears in large rounded clusters 10–12 cm (4–5 in) in diameter; the blooms are red (both calyx and corolla) and trumpet-shaped, ending in four rounded lobes, 2.5–3 cm (about 1 in) long. The plant blooms all year round.

Fruit: A black berry, but the plant is usually propagated from cuttings.

Comments: Ixora is an ornamental shrub cultivated throughout the Tropics. It prefers rich soil, full sun and lots of watering, and regular pruning. Related species cultivated in Cuban gardens include the yellow *I. lutea*; the white-flowering *I. thwaitessi* and *I. grandifolia*, which has larger leaves and flower clusters.

Jazmín de la Tierra

(Jazmín de Cinco Hojas, Jazmín de España, Jazmín, Jasmine)
Jasminum grandiflorum L.

Family: Oleaceae

Origin: Arabian peninsula; widely cultivated in tropical countries.

Plant type: A slender branching perennial vine, 3–5 m (10–16 ft) long; the stems are very narrow and slightly angular.

Leaves: Grow opposite one another and consist of seven to nine leaflets, the terminal one being the largest. The whole leaf is 5–10 cm (2–4 in) long.

Flowers: Clumps of flowers appear grouped in the leaf axils. The calyx is green, bell-shaped and tiny; the corolla is white with a long, thin tube 1.5–2.5 cm (½–1 in) long, culminating in four or more lobes. Very fragrant.

Fruit: A small, round, fleshy berry, purple or black when ripe, 5–8 mm (about ¼ in) diameter, single-seeded.

Comments: This vine is a popular ornamental plant in Cuba. It is renowned for its sedative properties: three flowers steeped in a cup of boiling water ensure restful sleep.

Jazmín Trompeta

(Bignonia de Río, Cape Honeysuckle)
Tecomaria capensis (Thunb.) Spach

Family: Bignoniaceae

Origin: South Africa.

Plant type: A bushy upright shrub.

Leaves: Alternate, compound, having five leaflets in two pairs with one larger one at the end, oval to round with serrated edges, dark green, 8–10 cm (3–4 in) long.

Flowers: Large, decorative bunches of six to eight trumpet-shaped, red-orange flowers, 3–4 cm (1–1½ in) long, in terminal and axillary positions. Blossoms from May to June.

Fruit: Not seen; propagated by cuttings.

Comments: This is a shrub widely cultivated in mild temperate to tropical countries. In Cuba its beautiful red-orange flowers make it a popular houseplant.

Júpiter

(Astronomía, Crape Myrtle, Crepe Myrtle, June Rose)
Lagerstroemia indica L.

Family: Lythraceae

Origin: Southeast Asia and Northern Australia.

Plant type: A small tree with rounded canopy, 3–4 m (10–13 ft) high.

Leaves: Alternate, elliptical with pointed or rounded tips, light green above and paler below; 1.5–6 cm (½–2¼ in) long and about 3 cm (1 in) wide.

Flowers: Very attractive with numerous flowers blooming in dense terminal panicles; the calyx is cup-shaped with six lobes; the six petals being flamboyantly frilly above their narrow bases, and white, pink, rosy-red, mauve or purple in colour according to the variety. Flowers from June to August.

Fruit: A diminutive woody seed pod opening into six to seven parts to allow the dispersal of the small, winged seeds.

Comments: Júpiter is used as an ornamental shrub in the majority of Cuban gardens and beside urban and country roads. The plant benefits from regular pruning after it has flowered.

Lágrimas de Cupido

(Lágrimas de Amor, Fountain Plant, Firecracker)
Russelia equisetiformis Schlecht. & Cham.

Family: Scrophulariaceae

Origin: Mexico.

Plant type: A profusely branching shrub up to 2 m (6½ ft) high with slender, arching stems. The branches and young growth are green and striated.

Leaves: Very small, disposed in whorls on the green stems

Flowers: The flowers appear in bunches of numerous small, red, tubular blooms with five rounded lobes, two of which are of a slightly smaller size and contain the stamens, thus making the flower asymmetrical; each flower is 2–3 cm (¾–1 in) long and about 1 cm (½ in) wide and contains a drop of nectar. The plant flowers all year round.

Fruit: A spherical brown seed pod less than 1 cm (½ in) diameter. May also be grown from cuttings.

Comments: Lágrimas de Cupido is commonly used in Cuba as a border plant; its flowers are often visited by butterflies and small hummingbirds.

Lila

(Ají de China, Ajicón)
Solanum havanense Jacq.

Family: Solanaceae

Origin: Cuba, Jamaica, Hispaniola.

Plant type: Shrub, 1–2 m (3–6½ ft) high.t

Leaves: Alternate, variable in shape, hairy on both sides, light green, 4–9 cm (1½–3½ in) long.

Flowers: These appear in sparse groups along the branches. The corolla is pale blue or lilac, forming a saucer shape with five lobes, separated half-way to their base, with pointed tips. Flowers all year round.

Fruit: Ovate, 1–2 cm (½–¾ in) long, dark purple, containing numerous seeds.

Comments: Lila grows wild on scrubland throughout Cuba. It is seldom cultivated but deserves attention for its delicate flowers and decorative purple fruits.

Lirio

(Lirio de Costa, Frangipán, Súcheli, Lirio Tricolor, Frangipani, Pagoda Tree, Temple Tree)
Plumeria rubra L.

Family: Apocynaceae

Origin: Central and South America.

Plant type: A deciduous, profusely branching tree or shrub with succulent stems and branches which contain a milky, latex-type sap.

Leaves: Grouped at the ends of the branches, obovate, with sharp tips and narrowed bases. The upper side is brilliant green with yellowish central and lateral veins, and a prominent marginal vein; the lower side is paler with a very prominent central vein; the total length is 12–50 cm (5–20 in) and up to 15 cm (6 in) wide. The leaves fall just before flowering takes place.

Flowers: Highly decorative, in large terminal clusters of 10 flowers or more, each one having five petals about 4 cm (1½ in) long, commonly with shading to yellow at their centres. The colours of the flowers include white, yellow, pink, rose-red, pinkish-yellow and purple; the flowers are strongly scented. Blossoms from May to August.

Fruit: The seed pods, formed of two long, cylindrical halves with sharp tips united at their bases and measuring 9–30 cm (3½–12 in) long, are full of small winged seeds. May also be propagated from large cuttings.

Comments: This is one of the most widely cultivated small ornamental trees in the Tropics. In some Asiatic countries it is used in cemeteries, but this is not the case in Cuba, where it is often planted near the sea.

Lirio de Sabana

(Lirio)
Plumeria clusioides Griseb.

WARNING: The milky sap is irritating to the eyes and poisonous if taken internally.

Family: Apocynaceae

Origin: Cuba, endemic.

Plant type: A branching shrub, 2–7 m (6½–23 ft) high.

Leaves: Grouped at the ends of the branches, long with rounded tips and narrow bases, with a prominent, yellow central vein and numerous parallel lateral ones; brilliant green above and paler below; 5–15 cm (2–6 in) long.

Flowers: Decorative, in terminal clusters of seven to ten flowers on a stalk, 15–20 cm (6–8 in) long; the white corolla, which measures 4–6 cm (1½–2¼ in) across, has five narrow lobes and is yellow at its centre. Subtly scented. Flowers from May to July.

Fruit: A seed pod divided into two cylindrical parts, 7–14 cm (2¾–5½ in) long, joined at their base, with sharp tips, containing numerous winged seeds that are dispersed when the dry fruit opens longitudinally.

Comments: Lirio de Sabana is an endemic shrub that is common in the woods and plains of central and eastern Cuba (especially around the cities of Santa Clara, Camagüey and Holguín). Its glossy leaves and delicate flowers make it a popular ornamental shrub.

Lirio de San Juan

(Lirio Sanjuanero, Spider Lily)
Hymenocallis latifolia (Mills.) M.J. Roem.

Family: Amaryllidaceae

Origin: Tropical America.

Plant type: An attractive plant which grows from a bulb to about 50 cm (20 in) tall.

Leaves: Arising in dense groups from the base of the plant, 35–50 cm (14–20 in) long and 4–5 cm (1½–2 in) wide, spear-shaped, bright green.

Flowers: Highly decorative, appearing in variable numbers (five to seven) on a flower stalk of the same length as the leaves. The flowers are tubular and terminate in six long, thin, white lobes with six long stamens united at their bases by a membranous cup-like white structure. Slightly scented. Blossoms June to August.

Fruit: A dry seed pod containing one or two green seeds.

Comments: This peculiar plant is used as ornamental for its unusual flowers which closely resemble large, decorative spiders. The Spanish name 'Lirio de San Juan' is due to the fact that the plant begins to flower around 24th June, St John's Day. Four native species of *Hymenocallis* grow in Cuba: *H. arenicola*, *H. caribaea*, *H. latifolia* and *H. praticola*, the latter being endemic to Central Cuba.

Lirio Turco

(Tawny Daylily)
Hemerocallis fulva L.

Family: Liliaceae

Origin: China and the Himalayas.

Plant type: A stemless tuber, 50–80 cm (20–32 in) high.

Leaves: Long and slender, 2–3 cm (¾–1 in) wide, light green.

Flowers: Very large and decorative, appearing in branched inflorescences; trumpet-shaped, terminating in six triangular orange-brown lobes with prominent central veins and crimson bands at their bases, 10–15 cm (4–6 in) in both length and width.

Fruit: Not seen; the plant is propagated asexually by division.

Comments: Lirio Turco is a common garden plant cultivated for its beautiful, long-lasting flowers. In Jamaica it has spread from its original domestic habitat to grow widely in the mountains.

Lluvia De Orquídeas

(Congea, Terciopelo)
Congea tomentosa Roxb.

Family: Lamiaceae

Origin: Malaysia; widely cultivated through-out the Tropics.

Plant type: A branching vine.

Leaves: Grow opposite one another from cylindrical stems, up to 13 cm (5 in) long, oval, the apex slightly pointed, very woolly, dark green.

Flowers: Very decorative, bunched at the ends of the branches, with three woolly light pink or lilac bracts, up to 4 cm (1½ in) long, arranged around every group of tiny white flowers. Blossoms from January to March.

Fruit: Not known in Cuba; it is propagated by cuttings.

Comments: Frequently used as an ornamental vine because of its decorative and long-lasting flowers, which are often used for arrangements.

Maena

(Mainereta, Vellosita, Mayenia, King's Mantle)
Thunbergia erecta (Benth.) T. Anderson

Family: Acanthaceae

Origin: Eastern Africa; widely cultivated in tropical and subtropical countries.

Plant type: A shrub growing to 1–1.5 m (3–5 ft) high.

Leaves: Growing opposite one another, variable in shape, dark green on both sides, 2–5 cm (¾–2 in) long.

Flowers: Trumpet-shaped, solitary flowers appear in the axils of the leaves, with two paler modified leaves covering the calyx. The tube of the flower is curved, yellow inside and white outside, and the five lobes of the corolla are tinted violet (in Cuba there is a variety with a white corolla, but this is very rare). Maena flowers all year round.

Fruit: A dry capsule.

Comments: Maena is commonly used for hedging because of its strongly vertical branches and abundant leaves. This plant responds well to pruning, so it is frequently used for topiary gardening.

Magnolia

(Large-flowered Magnolia)
Magnolia grandiflora L.

Family: Magnoliaceae

Origin: Southern North America.

Plant type: A tree with short branches that can grow to 25 m (80 ft) in its natural habitat; in Cuba it reaches 3–5 m (10–16 ft).

Leaves: The leaves are alternate, large, elliptical to ovate with sharp tips. They are thick and glossy, being deep brilliant green above and brown below, and measure about 10–20 cm (4–8 in) long and 7–10 cm (2¾–4 in) wide. Magnolia is an evergreen tree.

Flowers: The large single flowers have numerous ivory-coloured petals arranged in a spiral; they are slightly concave with rounded tips. The flowers, which appears in late summer, are strongly scented and grow to up to 25 cm (10 in) wide.

Fruit: The woody cone-like fruit has brilliant red seeds contained in cavities spirally disposed within the structure of the cone.

Comments: This magnificent tree is renowned for its large and fragrant flowers. Magnolia is among the most primitive living Angiosperm genera of trees that have undergone little evolutionary change for 100 million years, since the time when dinosaurs walked the Earth.

Majagua

(Majagua Azul, Blue Mahoe, Cuba Bark, Mountain Mahoe)
Talipariti elatum (Sw.) Fryxell

Synonym: *Hibiscus elatus* Sw.

Family: Malvaceae

Origin: Cuba and Jamaica

Plant type: A tall, leafy tree about 25 m (80 ft) high.

Leaves: Alternate, heart-shaped, bright green above and greyish on the lower surface which is slightly furry with strongly marked veins. The leaves are 8–20 cm (3–8 in) long and about the same width.

Flowers: Very decorative, the calyx having five lobes, 3–5 cm (1–2 in) long; the large, five-petalled corolla measures 8–12 cm (3–5 in). The stamens are fused into a column, only parting towards the outer end. The flowers are orange-yellow or orange-red, fading to deep crimson before they fall from the tree. Blooms in the dry season.

Fruit: A dry, hairy, spherical seed pod divided into five parts, containing several furry seeds.

Comments: Majagua is a common tree in Cuban rainforests and is cultivated for its high-quality timber. It is sometimes used as an ornamental for its numerous beautiful flowers and perennial foliage. Its bluish-green wood is used for building and making furniture. The flowers, roots and bark have numerous medicinal properties.

Marpacífico

(Amapola, Borrachona, Hibiscus)
Hibiscus rosa-sinensis L.

Family: Malvaceae

Origin: Tropical Asia.

Plant type: A shrub which sometimes achieves heights of 2–3 m (6–10 ft).

Leaves: Alternate, ovate, with widely serrated edges and long petioles, bright green, 15–20 cm (6–8 in) long and 7–10 cm (2¾–4 in) wide.

Flowers: Large and decorative, single, with a primary whorl of five or six linear sepals, a secondary whorl of trumpet-shaped, furry, light green, united sepals and a corolla formed of five brightly coloured petals, rounded at the apex and narrowing towards the base. The colour at the centre of the flower is intense; the numerous stamens are fused into a hollow column which protrudes from the flower and has numerous anthers and five stigmas at the top. The petals appear in various different colours: red, yellow, white, pink, etc., according to variety. There are also 'double' forms. Marpacífico flowers all year round; the flower lasts one day, wilting in the evening.

Fruit: Not seen. The plant is easily grown from cuttings.

Comments: Marpacífico is a very common flowering shrub in all Cuban gardens. The petals are boiled in water with sugar and gum arabic to make cough medicine.

Mariposa

(Mariposa Blanca, White Ginger Lily)
Hedychium coronarium J. König

Family: Zingiberaceae

Origin: Southern Asia.

Plant type: A perennial with leafy shoots of up to 1.5 m (5 ft) long, with subterranean rhizomes, growing in clumps. The leaf stalks sheath one another to form a shoot which covers the cane-like stem.

Leaves: Long, ovate with a sharp tip, 40 cm (16 in) long and up to 15 cm (6 in) wide, bright green on top and paler below.

Flowers: In terminal spikes formed by green bracts tightly disposed in a spiral pattern from which the pure white scented flowers arise in a shape similar to that of a butterfly ('mariposa' means butterfly); about 10 cm (4 in) wide. Flowers mainly in the rainy season.

Fruit: A brown spherical seed pod infrequently seen; the plant spreads by means of its rhizomes.

Comments: Although a native of southern Asia, Mariposa is the Cuban national flower and is very common not only in the island's gardens but also in the wild, in marshy soil beside rivers and in sunny areas. During the wars of independence in the nineteenth century, Cuban patriots used to hide their secret messages between the bracts or leaf sheaths of the Mariposa plant.

Marrullero

(Bejuco Marrullero, Bejuco Lechoso, Wild Vine)
Ipomoea tiliacea (Willd.) Choisy

Family: Convolvulaceae

Origin: Tropics of America.

Plant type: An annual vine growing to 1–2 m (3–6 ft).

Leaves: Alternate, heart-shaped, with sharp tips, 5–8 cm (2–3 in) long, containing milky sap.

Flowers: Marrullero has numerous pinkish-purple bell-shaped flowers with dark centres, 5–6 cm (2–2¼ in) long. Flowers all year round but mainly in December and January.

Fruit: A capsule containing four dark brown seeds.

Comments: A beautiful native plant commonly found in Cuba beside roads, in pastures, on riverbanks and in woods. It is said that this vine is the ancestor of the sweet potato, which was developed from Marrullero by means of selective cultivation.

Ojo de Poeta

(Anteojo de Poeta, Viuda, Black-eyed Susan)
Thunberghia alata Bojer ex Sims

Family: Acanthaceae

Origin: East and South Africa.

Plant type: A climbing herbaceous vine.

Leaves: Growing opposite one another, the leaves of Ojo de Poeta are triangular-oval with curved lobes at their edges; the bases are heart-shaped and the tips are pointed. The petioles are flat, deep green on their upper sides and paler below.

Flowers: Single flowers appear in the leaf axils and two modified leaves cover the lower part of the flower; the corolla is orange-yellow, tubular, with five extended lobes and a deep violet interior; the flower is about 2.5 cm (1 in) long and 5 cm (2 in) wide. Flowers all year round but principally in the winter.

Fruit: The seed pod has a pointed beak on its upper surface; it contains two to four seeds.

Comments: This curious vine can be found growing beside the road in damp areas, at low to medium altitudes, such as in Soroa. It is cultivated in temperate countries during warmer months as an annual. It was introduced into Cuba as an ornamental vine and later began to grow in the wild.

Orquídea Silvestre

(Bauhinia, Casco de Buey, Butterfly Tree, Orchid Tree, Ox or Bull Hoof Tree)
Bauhinia ssp.

Family: Caesalpiniaceae (Leguminosae)

Origin: India, Southeastern Asia.

Plant type: A small tree with a neat, rounded canopy.

Leaves: Alternate, large, broad, divided into two lobes (shaped like a bull's hoof), pale dull green, leathery, of differing sizes.

Flowers: Very decorative, appearing in racemes mainly at the ends of the branches. The blooms have a form similar to that of an orchid, having five purple, pink, lavender, yellow or white petals spotted with purple, red or yellow, with exposed stamens and pistils.

Fruit: Long, flat, bean-like seed pods ending in a beak and containing round, flat seeds.

Comments: These plants are cultivated throughout the island. The two most common species are *B. variegata* and *B. purpurea*. The genus name *Bauhinia* was dedicated by Linné (the father of botanical nomenclature) to the Swiss brothers Jean and Casper Bauhin, whose merits in botany were as identical as the two lobes of the leaves of this genus.

Ova

(Flor de Agua, Lirio de Agua, Ova Blanca, Ninfa, White Water Lily, Water Lily)
Nymphaea ampla (Salisb.) DC.

Family: Nymphaeaceae

Origin: Florida (USA), continental tropical America, West Indies.

Plant type: An aquatic plant with large, profusely growing, submerged rhizomes.

Leaves: Floating, rounded with a long, flexible petiole and serrated edges. The upper surface is bright green and waxy; the lower surface is red with prominent veins. The leaf grows up to 40 cm (16 in) wide, depending upon nutrients in the water.

Flowers: Very large and showy, protruding on stalks well above the surface of the water, generally white with several green sepals and 12 to 20 spear-shaped petals about 7–9 cm (2¾–3½ in) long, with numerous stamens at the centre. The flowers are very fragrant and appear throughout the year.

Fruit: A submerged berry; the plant can also be reproduced from the rhizome.

Comments: Ova is a native water lily, common in freshwater lagoons and ponds. Its beautiful, sweet-scented flowers open during the day. The plant varies in size according to the quantity of nitrogen present in its habitat, and according to the age of the plant. The pink-flowered species, *N. rosea*, is commonly cultivated in artificial ponds, in addition to the white, larger flowered *N. odorata*.

Palo Bobo

(Botija, Brazilian Rose, Silk Cotton, Buttercup Tree)
Cochlospermum vitifolium (Willd.) Spreng.

Family: Cochlospermaceae

Origin: Central and South America.

Plant type: A small deciduous tree, 5–12 m (16–40 ft) high with a grey trunk and branches.

Leaves: Alternate, the five-lobed leaves look rather like hands. Each of the lobes has a sharp tip, the bases are heart-shaped and the edges are serrated. The entire leaf measures 10–30 cm (4–12 in) wide and is deep green in colour. The tree sheds its leaves in December and the new shoots appear in April.

Flowers: Very decorative, grouped in terminal clusters of large, brilliant, silky yellow rose-like flowers with numerous petals and stamens, measuring 10–12 cm (4–5 in) across. Blossoms in February to March.

Fruit: The dark brown five-valved seed pod, 7–8 cm (about 3 in), across is filled with silky cotton fibres attached to the seeds. The plant is also easily reproduced by large cuttings.

Comments: Palo Bobo is a beautiful native flowering tree used as an ornamental in open spaces; it is also used to create hedges. The fibre found in the fruits is used for stuffing pillows.

Paraíso

(Indian Lilac, Pride of India)
Melia azedarach L.

> **WARNING:** The fruits are poisonous.

Family: Meliaceae

Origin: India.

Plant type: A tree with light foliage and rounded canopy. Straight trunk, about 15 m (50 ft) high, with rough brown bark, about 80 cm (32 in) in diameter when the tree is very old.

Leaves: Grouped at the end of branches, compound, formed of numerous leaflets with serrated edges, light green. About 70 cm (28 in) long.

Flowers: The fragrant, decorative mauve flowers appear grouped in small bunches. Blossoms during the dry season, from November to January.

Fruit: Oval, yellow, with a smooth surface; 2–4 cm (¾–1½ in) long. Poisonous to humans.

Comments: Paraíso is a popular, fast growing ornamental tree. It is naturalized in Cuba. The wood is used for furniture and sculpture and the branches and leaves are recommended for purifying baths by the devotees of certain Afro-Cuban religious cults. Paraíso is sometimes confused with the closely related species *Azadirachta indica*, known as the Neem Tree, although the canopy of the latter is much more dense.

Pentas

Pentas lanceolata (Forsk.) Defl.

Family: Rubiaceae

Origin: Tropical Africa and the Middle East.

Plant type: A small, freely branching shrub.

Leaves: Growing opposite one another, oval to spear-shaped with sharp tips, a hairy surface and prominent veins; bright, pale green above and darker green below, about 10 cm (4 in) long.

Flowers: Grouped in rounded, decorative clusters of dozens of small star-shaped flowers in tones of white, pale pink, pink and red.

Fruit: The small seed pods contain minute seeds; Pentas is mainly propagated by cuttings.

Comments: Pentas is very popular in tropical and temperate regions of the world owing to its beautifully coloured flowers and ease of propagation.

Peregrina

(Yuramira, Spicy Jatropha)
Jatropha integerrima Jacq.

Family: Euphorbiaceae

Origin: Greater Antilles.

Plant type: Slender shrub, 1–2 m (3–6½ ft) high.

Leaves: Variable in shape and size but usually 8–12 cm (3–5 in) long; bright green.

Flowers: Appearing in groups at the ends of the branches, each red flower is borne on a slender stalk 6–7 cm (2¼–2¾ in) long. The flowers have five petals, the two sexes being separate in different flowers, the male having curled yellow stamens and the female having a style divided into three parts. It blooms all year round.

Fruit: Pendulous greenish-brown seed pods about 15 mm (½ in) long and wide, with three cavities, each of which contains a seed.

Comments: Peregrina is a wild Cuban shrub cultivated as an ornamental because of its beautiful flowers and its graceful form.

Petrea

(Hiedra Morada, Flor de Papel, Bella Elvira, Bluebird Vine)
Petrea volubilis L.

Synonym: *Petrea arborea* Kunth
Family: Verbenaceae

Origin: Tropical America; widely cultivated as an ornamental plant.

Plant type: Shrubby vine with numerous branches.

Leaves: Leathery and rough on both sides, growing opposite one another, up to 12 cm (5 in) long, dull green on the upper side, lighter on the lower side.

Flowers: Appear in decorative bunches of numerous blooms up to 60 cm (2 ft) long from the axils of the leaves, the violet-blue calyx is approximately 2 cm (¾ in) long, with five lobes, the violet or white corolla is 1–2 cm (½–¾ in) long and also has five lobes. Flowers mainly in the dry season.

Fruit: Not known in Cuba or nearby islands (Puerto Rico and Virgin Islands). It is propagated from cuttings.

Comments: Petrea is one of the decorative vines used for ornamental purposes in Cuba. As blue is not a common colour among tropical flowers, it confers a touch of distinction upon the gardens in which it is cultivated.

Piñón

(Piñón de Pito, Piñón de Cerca, Piñón de Sombra, Búcare, Indian Coral Tree, Coral Bean, Cockspur)
Erythrina spp.

WARNING: The majority of the species are prickly.

Origin: Pantropical

Family: Fabaceae (Leguminosae).

Plant type: Profusely branched deciduous tree, with a rounded canopy, some with stout trunks. Height varies according to the species. Some grow to become very tall trees.

Leaves: Alternate, compound of three leaflets, the terminal one being larger than the two others that grow opposite one another; variably sized, light to deep green above and paler below.

Flowers: Large and decorative, in terminal or axillary racemes of pyramidal shape. The flowers are bright red or orange, almost tubular, and vary in size according to the species, frequently appearing during the dry season before the new leaf growth.

Fruit: The bean-like seed pods are reddish-brown and grow to between 10 cm (4 in) and 20 cm (8 in) long. The seeds contained within the pods are almost perfectly spherical. These plants are easily propagated from large cuttings.

Comments: This is a genus with more than 100 species in both the New and the Old Worlds. They are frequently used as ornamentals, as shade trees for coffee and cocoa plantations, and for hedging.

Piscuala

(Picuala)
Combretum indicum (L.) Jongkind

Synonym: *Quisqualis indica* L.

Family: Combretaceae

Origin: Tropical Asia.

Plant type: Branching vine.

Leaves: Growing in pairs opposite one another, oval with pointed tips, up to 17 cm (7 in) long and 7 cm (2¾ in) wide; the lower surface has a red, dusty coating.

Flowers: In bunches at the ends of the short branches. The calyx is tubular, very long and hairy; the corolla has five petals which are white or light pink when young and red at maturity; they measure 10–15 mm (about ½ in) long. Strongly scented; flowers throughout the year.

Fruit: Single-seeded oval fruits, with five wings, measuring about 3 cm (1 in) long.

Comments: Piscuala is an 'old-fashioned' plant in Cuban gardens, as it was widely used in the first half of the twentieth century for fences, gardens and courtyards. Nowadays it is less common in spite of its highly scented, abundant flowers. Its perfume has been likened to a mixture of apple, peach and pineapple fragrances. It is easily propagated by cuttings.

Platanillo

(Bandera Española)
Canna spp.

Family: Cannaceae

Origin: Central and South America.

Plant type: A herbaceous plant which achieves heights up to 1.5 m (5 ft). It does not have a real stem; the leaf stalks overlap one other to form a false one. Platanillo plants have subterranean rhizomes.

Leaves: Leaves of varying widths up to 50 cm (20 in) long with pointed tips, parallel veins and a waxy surface.

Flowers: Large flowers 10–15 cm (4–6 in) long in terminal bunches; the petals are wide or narrow depending upon the species, and run the gamut of colours from red to creamy-white, through yellow, red, pale yellow, deep pink and orange. Blossoms all year round.

Fruit: When it is present (as in *Canna coccinea*), is a brown, rough, dry seed pod with three cavities containing several black, round seeds of 0.5 cm in diameter.

Comments: Cannaceae is a small family of about fifty or more species that were hybridized some time ago to obtain the current species, the most common of which are red. They provide a splash of colour in gardens, and one may sometimes see them growing in damp soil in areas where previously established gardens have run wild.

Plátano Cimarrón

(Heliconia, Wild Banana, Bird of Paradise)
Heliconia spp.

Family: Heliconiaceae
Origin: Tropical America.

Plant type: Tall to medium-sized herbaceous plants growing from rhizomes; the 'stems' are formed by the bases of the leaves, as in the Banana plant.

Leaves: Very large, with leaf blades 1 m (3¼ ft) or more in length and 25–40 cm (10–16 in) wide. A prominent central vein runs along the leaf, with numerous lateral veins branching from it; the petioles grow to 1 m (about 3 ft) or more; the surface of the leaf is smooth and somewhat waxy, especially when young.

Flowers: The real flowers are tiny, but they are contained in large, brightly coloured structures made up of rigid, waxy or velvety bracts which grow

alternately from the 'stem'. Yellow, orange, purple and red combine in these fantastic forms to resemble exotic birds – hence the common name 'Bird of Paradise'. The different species of the plant bloom at different times of the year but mostly during the rainy season.

Fruit: Tiny, deep blue seed pod with three hard seeds; however, the plant is propagated mainly by rhizome division.

Comments: These exotic ornamental plants are used mainly for flower arrangements. More than 40 species exist in tropical American countries and they are particularly common in the Caribbean. In Cuba, the native Plátano Cimarrón, *H. caribaea*, grows in the humid forests of the Sierra Maestra mountain range at the eastern end of the island.

Rabo de Gato

(Califa, Acalifa Japonesa, Monkey Tail, Chenille Plant)
Acalypha hispida Burm. f.

Family: Euphorbiaceae

Origin: Southeastern Asia

Plant type: Shrub about 2 m (6½ ft) high.

Leaves: Alternate, heart-shaped with pointed tips, bright green with prominent yellow veins on the surface and slightly serrated edges; 10–20 cm (4–8 in) long.

Flowers: The plant's pendulous furry red inflorescences up to 20 cm (8 in) long, similar in appearance to cats' tails, are made up of minute, red petal-less flowers. The plant blooms all year round.

Fruit: Not seen. Asexually propagated in Cuba.

Comments: Rabo de Gato is a beautiful shrub common in gardens throughout the Caribbean. It maintains its red-green combination of flowers and leaves all year round and needs no special care.

Reina de las Flores

(Júpiter de la Reina, Queen of Flowers, Pride of India)
Lagerstroemia speciosa (L.) Pers.

Family: Lythraceae

Origin: Tropical Asia.

Plant type: A medium-sized deciduous tree which can grow to 15 m (50 ft) high. Straight, light brown, smooth trunk and rounded canopy.

Leaves: Growing alternately from the stem, elliptical to spear-shaped with sharp tips, dull green above and paler green below with yellow veining; up to 15–20 cm (6–8 in) long and 5–6 cm (about 2 in) wide.

Flowers: Very showy, appearing in large numbers in generous, light grey terminal panicles of pale pink flowers that fade to dark pink during the day. The flowers have a cup-shaped, pale grey, slightly hairy calyx with six star-like lobes; the corolla has six curled petals and a very narrow base. Numerous pink stamens appear at the centre of the flower, which measures approximately 8 cm (3 in) in diameter. Blossoms from May to August.

Fruit: The spherical, woody, brown seed pod, 2–3 cm (¾–1 in) in diameter, opens in six or seven parts to release the small, winged seeds.

Comments: This is a spectacular tree when it is in flower, with an outstanding display of different tones of pink in its large clusters of blossom. In its region of origin the wood is highly prized for its quality, being used for boat construction, furniture, flooring, etc.

Roble Amarillo

(Yellow Poui)
Tabebuia chrysantha (Jacq.) G. Nicholson

Family: Bignoniaceae

Origin: Tropical America.

Plant type: A deciduous tree with rounded-narrow canopy and straight trunk with furrowed light brown bark. Up to 15 m (50 ft) high, less in Cuba.

Leaves: Alternate, compound, with five to seven large leaflets, 15–25 cm (6–10 in) long suspended from long petioles, light green with coppery fur on both sides; this fur also appears on new growth and on the petioles.

Flowers: Highly decorative; the clusters of numerous golden-yellow flowers grow from the ends of the branches and twigs. They are trumpet-shaped, about 6–7 cm (about 2½ cm) long and wide with five lobes with frilled edges. The flowers appear before the growth of leaves, in March to April.

Fruit: The hanging, brown seed pod of up to 40 cm (16 in) long opens longitudinally when ripe to permit the dispersal of the winged seeds by the wind.

Comments: This is one of the most beautiful flowering trees in the Caribbean: it is a blaze of golden-yellow blossom when in flower. The Roble Amarillo is the Venezuelan national tree.

Roble de Yugo

(Roble blanco)
Tabebuia angustata Britton

Family: Bignoniaceae

Origin: Cuba, Jamaica.

Plant type: A deciduous tree growing up to 12 m (40 ft). Straight trunk, about 35 cm (14 in) in diameter. Canopy is narrow and sparse; the furrowed bark is brown with grey patches.

Leaves: Alternate, made up of three to seven finger-shaped leaflets. The leaf as a whole is 5–18 cm (2–7 in) long, bright green, stiff and spear-shaped, with a leathery surface and a sharp tip.

Flowers: Highly showy, appearing after the leaves have fallen in clusters of up to 40 pale pink, white or mauve flowers growing at the ends of the branches and twigs. The individual flowers are 7 cm (2¾ in) long and 7 cm (2¾ in) wide. They are asymmetrically trumpet-shaped with yellow throats and five lobes which are frilled at the edges. Blossoms from May to June.

Fruit: A brown pod, 10–25 cm (4–10 in) long, which opens when ripe to release the seeds.

Comments: Roble de Yugo is a beautiful native tree common on the banks of rivers and creeks, in swamps and woods at lower altitudes. Its timber is used for making tools. It is also popular as an ornamental due to its beautiful pale-pink blossoms; it may be seen throughout the city of Havana.

Roble Maquiligua

(Roble Magriña, Pink Poui, Pink Tecoma, White Cedar, Pink Trumpet Tree)
Tabebuia heterophylla (DC.) Britton

Synonym: *Tabebuia pentaphylla* (L.) Hemsl.

Family: Bignoniaceae

Origin: Tropical America.

Plant type: A deciduous tree which can grow up to 18 m (60 ft) high, usually less in Cuba.

Leaves: Alternate, compound with two to five leaflets forming leaves looking rather like an open hand, varies widely in shape and size, bright green above and paler below.

Flowers: The trumpet-shaped pink flowers, which appear when the tree is leafless, are arranged in bunches of numerous (35 to 40) blooms, 7–10 cm (2¾–4 in) long. Blossoms erratically from April to August.

Fruit: The long seed pod, which measures about 20 cm by 0.6 cm (8 in by ¼ in), opens when ripe to permit the dispersal of the winged seeds.

Comments: This magnificent tree was introduced into Cuba from Mexico and Central America during the first half of the twentieth century. Fallen blossoms often cause the ground surrounding the tree to look like a pink carpet. In other countries, its wood is used for furniture, and the trees are planted for shade on coffee plantations.

Romerillo de Playa

(Wedelia, Creeping Ox-eye, Marigold)
Wedelia trilobata (L.) Hitchc.

Family: Asteraceae (Compositae)

Origin: Tropical America.

Plant type: Herb with spreading and creeping branches of 2 m (6½ ft) long or more.

Leaves: Opposite, obovate, triple-lobed with serrated edges; the deep green leaves measure 2–12 cm (¾–5 in) long and 2–7 cm (¾–2¾ in) wide and have furry surfaces.

Flowers: The single flower heads appear on stalks, 2.5 cm (1 cm) to 14 cm (5½ in) long; the calyx is cup-shaped and the inflorescence above it is composed of yellow petals terminating in several short, irregular divisions and surrounding the true flowers, tiny yellow structures arranged in a dense mass at the centre of the flower head.

Fruit: Numerous small seeds about 5 mm (¼in) in diameter are found in the dried structures of the flower heads.

Comments: This is a common native plant which thrives near the coast and in damp soil inland. Its golden flower heads and rapid growth make it useful for ground cover.

Saltaperico

(Dinamita, Fulminante, Duppy Gun)
Ruellia tuberosa L.

Family: Acanthaceae

Origin: Tropical America (including southern USA).

Plant type: Bushy herb, 10–50 cm (4–20 in) high, straight stem, simple or branched, with thick roots.

Leaves: Up to 10 cm (4 in) long, the apex is round and the base is narrow, dull green.

Flowers: Each plant produces several bell-shaped blue flowers measuring 4–6 cm (1½–2¼ in) long. Blooms all year round.

Fruit: A cylindrical seed pod, 1.5–2 cm (½–¾ in) long, containing 10 to 12 tiny seeds that are flung out when the dry fruit opens.

Comments: A beautiful wild plant which grows all over the island in swamps and grasslands. There are several related species with similar blue flowers.

Tararaco

(Azucena de México, Amaryllis)
Hippeastrum puniceum (Lam.) Voss

Family: Amaryllidaceae

Origin: South America.

Plant type: The plant grows from a round, brown, scaly bulb, 4–5 cm (1½–2 in) in diameter.

Leaves: Bright green, sword-shaped, 20–40 cm (8–16 in) long and up to 5 cm (2 in) wide, narrow at the apex.

Flowers: Appear on a hollow greenish-yellow stalk about 25 cm (10 in) long. Each stalk bears two to four trumpet-shaped flowers, 9–12 cm (3½–5 in) wide and up to 20 cm (8 in) long, with six petals curling backwards at the tips; they are brilliant red with greenish-white interiors. Blossoms May to June.

Fruit: A spherical seed pod with three valves containing numerous round, flat, brown, papery seeds.

Comments: Tararaco is frequently cultivated in gardens or in pots. Its beauty and the way in which it remains fresh for several days after being cut makes it very popular for flower arrangements.

Tulipán Africano

(Espatodea, African Tulip Tree, Tulip Tree)
Spathodea campanulata Beauv.

WARNING: The fruit of this tree is poisonous.

Family: Bignoniaceae

Origin: Tropical Africa.

Plant type: A perennial tree 15–25 m (50–80 ft) tall, with a straight, smooth, grey trunk.

Leaves: Large, up to 60 cm (2 ft) long, made up of four to eight pairs of leaflets, deep olive green.

Flowers: Very showy, asymmetrical bell-shaped flowers up to 12 cm (5 in) long, grouped in circular racemes at the ends of the branches outside the canopy; scarlet to orange. The unopened flower buds contain watery liquid. Blossoms all year round, mostly in the dry season.

Fruit: The seed pods are 20 cm (8 in) long and contain winged seeds; the fruit is highly poisonous.

Comments: This beautiful ornamental tree may be seen all over Cuba. It was introduced into the island at the beginning of the twentieth century by the Experimental Agronomic Station and has become naturalized, growing widely on plains and in the mountains, mainly in the Western provinces.

Varía

(Baría, Varía Negra, Varía Prieta, Spanish Elm, Panichellum)
Cordia gerascanthus L.

Family: Boraginaceae

Origin: Central America and the Caribbean.

Plant type: A leafy perennial tree about 30 m (100 ft) high.

Leaves: Alternate, dark green leaves, spear-shaped to oblong with sharp tips, 5–12 cm (2–5 in) long.

Flowers: Very decorative, in dense clusters of fragrant white blossoms with tubular corollas terminating in five rounded lobes, 2–3 cm (¾–1 in) long. The flowers fade to a pale, papery brown when mature and remain attached to the tree for some time. Blooms March to May.

Fruit: Dry seed pods to which the papery petals remain attached, performing the function of wings for wind dispersal.

Comments: Varía is one of the most beautiful Cuban native trees. It is frequently used in streets (a particularly attractive example may be seen in 23rd Street in Havana) and parks. Varía is resistant to drought, as its natural habitat is the dry coastal forest of Cuba.

Vicaria

(Vicaria Blanca, Periwinkle, Ramgoat Rose)
Catharanthus roseus (L.) G. Don.

Synonym: *Vinca rosea* L.

Family: Apocynaceae

Origin: Madagascar.

Plant type: Small branching shrub, 30–50 cm (12–20 in) high.

Leaves: Growing opposite one another, elliptical to oblong, leathery, bright green with a pale central vein; up to 8 cm (3 in) long.

Flowers: Grow from the ends of the branches, trumpet-shaped, with five white or pink rounded lobes at the front edge, the throat of the flowers being dark lilac to red, 2.5–4 cm (1–1½ in) long. Blossoms all year round.

Fruit: Oblong seed pod consisting of two parts, resembling small horns, 2–3 cm (¾–1 in) long, which open when dry to disperse numerous small seeds.

Comments: Vicaria is one of the most frequently cultivated plants in Cuban gardens and public spaces and is useful in the treatment of eye infections.

Vomitel Colorado

(Vomitel, Geiger Tree, Scarlet Cordia, Anaconda, Geranium Tree)
Cordia sebestena L.

Family: Boraginaceae

Origin: Tropical America.

Plant type: A shrub or small tree growing up to 8 m (26 ft) high, with a dense, rounded canopy.

Leaves: Growing alternately, the leaves are of a rounded oval shape with pointed tips. They have a rough surface texture, and are dark, dull green above and pale green on their lower surfaces. They measure 9–16 cm (3½–6 in) long and 5–14 cm (2–5½ in) wide.

Flowers: Decorative, in rounded terminal clusters about 10 to 15 flowers each; bright red-orange, trumpet-shaped, terminating in six round, flat lobes measuring 2.5 cm (1 in) across. Blossoms during the rainy season.

Fruit: Fleshy, white, plum-like fruits about 2.5 cm (1 in) in diameter; fragrant and sweet, with one to three seeds.

Comments: Vomitel Colorado is a small but beautiful perennial native tree and is frequently planted as an ornamental. It occurs naturally in coastal vegetation and is thus resistant to drought. Its fruits may be eaten either raw or cooked, but they are not particularly tasty. Its wood is used for fine furniture and musical instruments.

Orquídeas

(Orchids)

The Orchid is known as the Queen of Flowers due to its regal beauty, just as the palm is known as the Prince of Trees.

Orchids may be found all over the world, from coasts to mountains, from equatorial to temperate regions and even further north. There is however no doubt that tropical climates constitute the orchid's real kingdom: of the 25 000 or more species that are known, 85% are found in tropical and subtropical regions. A further 30 000 hybrid orchids have been created by breeders unable to resist the temptation to multiply, accentuate and increase the beauty of the orchid.

Orchids are herbaceous plants. Some are terrestrial, others are epiphytes and many are climbers. The epiphytic and climbing forms are common in tropical rainforests, whilst the terrestrial species grow in drier and more temperate ecosystems. Many species of orchid possess enlarged stems, known as pseudobulbs, in which reserves of water and nutrients are held.

These plants vary widely in size, colour and shape, but they have a basic pattern of floral architecture that always remains the same: an outer whorl of three petals, followed by an inner whorl of three petals, two of which are identical, with the third being much larger and more showy, named the 'labellum' (lip). Appearing in numerous different shapes and colours, this forms the 'throat' of the flower in which is contained the fusion between the stamens and the pistil, referred to as the 'column' of the flower. This basic structure is repeated in every orchid, from the very smallest (a few millimetres in size) to the large, flamboyant blooms so beloved of florists.

The floral morphology of orchids is closely related to their pollinators, and each species of orchid, or group of closely related species, has its own specific pollinating insect.

In Cuba, over 300 species of native orchids have been registered, of which an estimated 32% are endemic. The following six species, three of which are cultivated and three native or naturalized, may be found in Cuba either in the wild or in such collections as the Soroa Orchid Garden in the province of Pinar del Río.

Candelaria

(Orquidea de San Miguel)
Bletia purpúrea (Lam.) DC.

A terrestrial orchid of less than 1 m (3 ft) high. The pseudobulbs are spherical and the leaves are long, folded, spear-shaped, with sharp tips and veined on their lower surfaces. The purple flowers are grouped in panicles. The sepals are spear-shaped and pointed and the petals are similar, with a triple-lobed labellum. The lateral lobes of the labellum are curved, the central one being the shortest. Candelaria flowers all year round, but most profusely in April, and grows all over Cuba, Florida, the Bahamas and the Greater Antilles, Central and South America. This beautiful flower is the symbol of the Biosphere Reserve of Sierra del Rosario, in the Cuban province of Pinar del Rio.

Orquídea Catleya

Cattleya labiata Lindl.

An epiphyte, this large cultivated plant has leathery leaves and very decorative flowers, 12–15 cm (5–6 in) in diameter, grouped together in pairs or in larger numbers. The sepals and petals are bright pink; the latter are broad and have a waxy surface. The labellum is large and deep violet, the throat is yellow. Numerous hybrids of *Cattleya labiata* are cultivated by amateurs. The species originated in Trinidad and Brazil. Blossoms in winter (November to January).

Orquídea Cimarrona

Broughtonia cubensis (Ldl.) Cogniaux

An epiphytic native plant with numerous thick aerial roots, closely grouped pseudobulbs and rigid, leathery leaves. The flowers appear in terminal inflorescences with white sepals and broad white petals. The labellum is large, tinged with purple and yellow, and has a frilly edge. This orchid may be found in coastal woodland. The genus *Broughtonia* is endemic to the Antilles, and the species *cubensis* is endemic to Cuba. Blossoms most profusely in January.

Orquídea Monja

Phaius tankervilliae (Banks & L´Héritier) Blume

A terrestrial orchid with numerous spear-shaped leaves that can grow to over a metre high from its fleshy rhizome. Its flowers appear in bunches, the petals being white on their undersides and yellowish brown above, with a triple-lobed labellum, in which the side lobes are white above and maroon on their lower surfaces, enveloping the column, and the central lobe is maroon, rounded, with flashes of white and yellow appearing in the throat of the flower. Naturalized in Cuba and the other islands of the Caribbean. Blossoms March to April.

Orquídea del Sol

(Arequita)
Spathoglottis plicata Blume

A terrestrial plant with numerous thin, folded leaves, 80–100 cm (32–40 in) tall. Its tall racemes bear numerous small flowers which vary from pink to purple and are produced in succession. The sepals are extended and the petals are oval. The labellum has three lobes, the central one bearing a yellow spot. This orchid, which originated in Southeast Asia, blossoms all year round and is naturalized in Cuba, Puerto Rico and Hispaniola.

Vanda

Vanda teres (Roxb.) Lindl.

A decorative climbing orchid with round stems and leaves, ascending in trees up to 2 m (6½ ft) by means of aerial roots. The flowers are not profuse, but they are large and beautiful, about 6 cm (2¼ in) across, with white sepals tinged with pink. The large petals are magenta, the lobed labellum is carmine red and the throat is orange. The species is native to Northeastern India and Burma and it blossoms all year round.

Glossary

Alternate: describes leaves alternating up a stem, growing first from one side then the other.

Angiosperm: a plant with seeds enclosed in an ovary.

Annual: a plant that completes its life cycle within a single year.

Anther: the part of a stamen that contains pollen.

Appendage: small protrusion on a sepal or petal.

Asexual reproduction: a form of reproduction without fertilization.

Axil: the upper angle between a leaf and a stem.

Axillary: growing from an axil.

Bract: leaf or scale below calyx.

Calyx: whorl of leaves forming outer case of bud or envelope of flower.

Canopy: the branches and foliage of a tree.

Capsule: a dry seed-case opening when ripe by parting of valves.

Compound leaf: a leaf formed by sub-units known as 'leaflets'.

Corolla: whorl of modified leaves known as petals, separate or joined, forming inner envelope of flower.

Deciduous: describes plants that shed their leaves seasonally.

Endemic: applied to a species or group of organisms which occur naturally in a restricted geographical region.

Epiphyte: a plant that naturally grows upon another plant but does not derive any nourishment from it.

Inflorescence: complete flower head of a plant.

Leaflet: one of the parts of which a compound leaf is composed.

Obovate: ovate with narrower end at base.

Opposite: describes leaves growing from the main stem in pairs, one opposite the other.

Ovate: egg-shaped.

Panicle: loose irregular type of compound inflorescence.

Perennial: a plant that lives for more than two years.

Petiole: slender stalk joining leaf-blade to stem.

Pistil: the female parts of a flower.

Raceme: a type of inflorescence in which the flowers are arranged along an axis.

Rhizome: a horizontal underground stem that bears small roots.

Sepal: modified leaves that form the calyx of a flower.

Sheath: the lowest part of the petiole, enveloping the stem.

Spike: a type of inflorescence in which a long stem bears many stalkless flowers.

Stamen: the male organ of a flower, composed of filament and anther.

Style: the upper part of the female organ of the flower, usually found within a ring of petals.

Terminal: at the end or tip.

Whorl: ring of leaves or other organs around the stem.

Bibliography

Adams, C. D. (1972) *Flowering Plants of Jamaica*. University of West Indies, Mona, Jamaica.
Anonymous [Royal Botanic Gardens Kew] (1997) *Index Kewensis 2.0* [CD-ROM]. Oxford University Press, Oxford.
Barwick, M. (2004) *Tropical and Subtropical Trees: An Encyclopedia*. Timber Press, Portland.
Borhidi, A. (1991) *Phytogeography and Vegetation Ecology of Cuba*. Akadémiai Kiadó, Budapest.
Clement, I. D., Clement, V. W., Walsingham, F. G., Weeks, J. W. & Weeks, K. C. (1954) *Guide to the Most Interesting Plants of the Atkins Garden*. Harvard University, Atkins Garden and Laboratory, Cienfuegos.
Ellison, D.P. (1995) *Cultivated Plants of the World*. Flora Publications International Pty Ltd. Brisbane.
Howard, R. A. (1988–1989) *Flora of the Lesser Antilles, Leeward and Windward Islands*, Vol. 4–6. Arnold Arboretum of Harvard University, Jamaica Plain.
Mujica Pércz, E. (2000) *Géneros de orquídeas cubanas*. Editorial 'Félix Varela', La Habana.
León, Hno. & Alain, Hno. [Liogier, H. A.] (1946–1969) *Flora de Cuba, Contribuciones Ocasional Museo de Natural Historia Colegio 'De La Salle'* 8, 10, 13, 16, Suplemento.
Roig y Mesa, J. T. (1963) *Diccionario botánico de nombres vulgares cubanos*, 3rd ed., 1–2. Editorial Científico-Técnica, La Habana.
Roig y Mesa, J. T. (1974) *Plantas medicinales, aromáticas o venenosas de Cuba*, 2nd ed. Editorial Científico-Técnica, La Habana.
Seddon, S. A. & Lennox, G. W. (1980) *Trees of the Caribbean*. Macmillan Education, London.
Various (1998–2003) *Flora de la República de Cuba*. Koeltz Scientific Books, Konigstein.
Zulueta, M. E. & Moreno, H. (eds) (1999) *Cuba y sus árboles*. Editoriales Academia y Caja Madrid, La Habana & Madrid.

Index of Common names

Abrojo de la Florida 1
Acalifa Japonesa 85
Achiote 14
Adelfa 2
African Tulip Tree 93
Aguinaldo 4
Aguinaldo Amarillo 3
Aguinaldo Blanco 4
Aguinaldo de Campanilla 4
Aguinaldo de Pascuas 4
Aguinaldo Morado 21
Ají de China 61
Ajicón 61
Ajo De Jardín 5
Alamanda 6
Algodón 7
Alpinia 8
Amapola 70
Amaryllis 92
Ambarina 39
Amor y Celos 13
Anaconda 96
Angel's Tears/Trumpet 20
annuals, Brujita 17
Anteojo de Poeta 73
Anthurium 9
Anturio 9
Apple Blossom Cassia 27
Arbol Cardenal 25
Arequita 102
Asistasia 10
Astronomía 59
Ave del Paraíso 11
Azucena de México 92
Azulejo 35

Bandera Española 83
Baría 94
Bauhinia 74
Bauhinia Roja 12
Bayoneta 36
Beach Morning Glory 15
Bejuco Lechoso 72
Bejuco Marrullero 72
Bella Elvira 80
Bella Hortensia 1
Bien vestida 13
Bienvestido 13

Bignonia de Río 58
Bija 14
Bird of Paradise 84
Bird of Paradise Flower 11
Black-Eyed Susan 73
Blue Mahoe 69
Blue Trumpet Vine 38
Bluebird Vine 80
Boca de Dragón 30
Boniato de Playa 15
Borrachona 70
Botija 76
Botón de Oro 52
Bottle Brush Tree 19
Bougainvillea 16
Brazilian Rose 76
Bruja 17
Brujita 17
Búcare 81
bulbs, Tararaco 92
Bull Hoof Tree 74
Buttercup Flower 6
Buttercup Tree 76
Butterfly Tree 74

Caliandra 18
Caliandra Roja 18
Califa 85
Calistemon 19
Campana 20
Campana Gallega 21
Caña Fistula 23
Caña Mexicana 22
Cañafístola 23
Cañafistula Cimarrona 24
Cañandonga 24
Candelaria 98
Candlestick 54
Cañuela Santa 22
Cape Honeysuckle 58
Cape Jessamine 51
Cardenal 25
Carolina 26
Casco de Buey 74
Casia de Java 27
Casia Nodosa 27
Chenille Plant 85
Christmas Pops 4

Claro de Luna 40
Clavelón 41
Clerodendro 28
Clerodendro rojo 28
climbers
  Bauhinia Roja 12
  Bougainvillea 16
  Clerodendro 28
  Fausto 38
  Flor de la Luna 40
  see also vines
Clock Vine 38
Cockspur 81
Cojate 30
Cola de Camarón 29
Cola de Camarón Amarilla 29
Colonia 30
Congea 66
Copetuda 41
Coral Bean 81
Coral Hibiscus 37
Coral Shower 24
Coral Vegetal 31
Coral Vine 32
Coralillo 32
Coralillo Rosado 32
Corazón de Jesús 9
Corona de Cristo 33
Cosmos 34
Cotton 7
Crape Myrtle 59
Creeping Ox-eye 90
Crepe Myrtle 59
Crown-of-Thorns 33
Cuba Bark 69
Cucharillo 46

Dinamita 91
Duppy Gun 91

Embeleso 35
Escabiosa 39
Escobilla Morisca 39
Espatodea 93
Espino 36
Estrelizia 11

Falso Sauce 19

Farolito Chino 37
Fausto 38
Fernandina 39
Firecracker 60
Flamboyán 44
Flamboyant 44
Flame of the Forest 56
Flame Tree 44
Flamingo Flower 9
Flor de Agua 75
Flor de Barbero 6
Flor de Cera 38
Flor de Clavo 48
Flor de la Luna 40
Flor de la 'Y' 40
Flor de Muerto 41
Flor de Nieve 42
Flor de Papel 16, 80
Flor de Pascua 43
Fountain Plant 60
Framboyán 44
Framboyán Amarillo 45
Frangipán/Frangipani 62
Frijolillo 46
Fruta de Iguana 50
Fulminante 91

Galán 48
Galán de Día 47
Galán de Noche 48
Galán Morado 49
Garbancillo 50
Gardenia 51
Geiger Tree 96
Geranium Tree 96
Ginger 30
Ginger Lily 8
Goat Foot 15
Golden Candles 29
Golden Dewdrop 50
Gout plant 31
Gracia de Dios 33
Granito de Oro 52
Guacamaya 53
Guacamaya Francesa 54
Guacamayón 54
Guamá Piñón 46
Guava 55
Guayaba/Guayabo 55

Heart Flower 9
Heliconia 84

herbaceous plants
  Anturio 9
  Asistasia 10
  Ave del Paraíso 11
  Boniato de Playa 15
  Caña Mexicana 22
  Flor de Muerto 41
  Platanillo 83
  Plátano Cimarrón 84
herbs
  Cosmos 34
  Fernandina 39
  Romerillo de Playa 90
  Saltaperico 91
Hibiscus 70
Hiedra Morada 80
Hierba de los Herpes 54
Horse Cassia 24

Indian Coral Tree 81
Indian Laburnum 23
Indian Lilac 77
Ixora 56
Ixora roja 56

Japanese Hibiscus 37
Jasmine 57
Jazmín 57
Jazmín Azul 35
Jazmín de Cinco Hojas 57
Jazmín de Día 47
Jazmín de España 57
Jazmín de la Tierra 57
Jazmín del Cabo 51
Jazmín del Vedado 42
Jazmín Trompeta 58
June Rose 59
Júpiter 59
Júpiter Cimarrón 50
Júpiter de la Reina 86
Juravaina 46

King-of-the-Forest 54
King's Mantle 67

Lágrimas de Amor 60
Lágrimas de Cupido 60
Large-flowered Magnolia 68
Lila 61
Lila de las Antillas 49
Lirio 62, 63
Lirio de Agua 75

Lirio de Costa 62
Lirio de Sabana 63
Lirio de San Juan 64
Lirio Sanjuanero 64
Lirio Tricolor 62
Lirio Turco 65
Lluvia De Orquídeas 66

Maena 67
Magnolia 68
Mainereta 67
Majagua 69
Majagua Azul 69
Marigold 41, 90
Mariposa 71
Mariposa Blanca 71
Marpacífico 70
Marpacífico chino 37
Marrullero 72
Mata-Ratón 13
Mayenia 67
Mexican Creeper 32
Mimosa 18
Monkey Tail 85
Moon flower 40
Mountain Mahoe 69

Nabasco 48
Night Ipomoea 40
Ninfa 75
No-Me-Olvides 50
Nodding Cassia 27

Ojo de Poeta 73
Oleander 2
Orchid Tree 74
Orchids 97–103
Orquídea Catleya 99
Orquídea Cimarrona 100
Orquídea de San Miguel 98
Orquídea del Sol 102
Orquídea Monja 101
Orquídea Silvestre 74
Orquídeas 97–103
Ova 75
Ova Blanca 75
Ox Hoof Tree 74

Pagoda Tree 62
Palo Basigato 19
Palo Bobo 76
Panichellum 94
Paraíso 77

Pea Tree 13
Peacock Flower 53
Pentas 78
perennials
    Ajo De Jardín 5
    Alpinia 8
    Colonia 30
    Mariposa 71
    Peregrina 79
    Periwinkle 95
    Petrea 80
    Picuala 82
    Pigeon Berry 50
    Pink Poui 89
    Pink Tecoma 89
    Pink Trumpet Tree 89
    Piñón 81
    Piñón Amoroso 13
    Piñón de Cerca 81
    Piñón de Pito 81
    Piñón de Sombra 81
    Piñón Florido 13
    Piscuala 82
    Platanillo 83
    Plátano Cimarrón 84
    Poinciana 44
    Poinsettia 43
    Potato Bush 21
    Pride of Barbados 53
    Pride of Guatemala 25
    Pride of India 77, 86

Queen of Flowers 86
Quick Stick 13

Rabo de Gato 85
Rain Flower 17
Ramgoat Rose 95
Red Head Calliandra 18
Reina de las Flores 86
Ringworm Shrub 54
Roble Amarillo 87
Roble blanco 88
Roble de Yugo 88
Roble Magriña 89
Roble Maquiligua 89
Romerillo de Playa 90
Rosa Francesca 2
Royal Poinciana 44

Saltaperico 91
Santa Rita 56
Scarlet Cordia 96

Shaving Brush Tree 26
Shower of Gold 23
Shrimp Plant 29
shrubs
    Adelfa 2
    Algodón 7
    Bauhinia Roja 12
    Bija 14
    Bougainvillea 16
    Caliandra Roja 18
    Campana 20
    Campana Gallega 21
    Cola de Camarón 29
    Coral Vegetal 31
    Corona de Cristo 33
    Embeleso 35
    Farolito Chino 37
    Flor de Pascua 43
    Galán de Día 47
    Galán de Noche 48
    Galán Morado 49
    Garbancillo 50
    Gardenia 51
    Granito de Oro 52
    Guacamaya 53
    Guacamaya Francesa 54
    Ixora 56
    Jazmín Trompeta 58
    Lágrimas de Cupido 60
    Lila 61
    Lirio 62
    Lirio de Sabana 63
    Maena 67
    Marpacífico 70
    Pentas 78
    Peregrina 79
    Rabo de Gato 85
    Vicaria 95
    Vomitel Colorado 96
Silk Cotton 76
Sky Flower 50
South African Leadwort 35
Spanish Bayonet 36
Spanish Dagger 36
Spanish Elm 94
Spicy Jatropha 79
Spider Lily 64
Spiral Flag 22
Súcheli 62
Susana Blanca 42

Tararaco 92

Tawny Daylily 65
Temple Tree 62
Terciopelo 66
trees
    Abrojo de la Florida 1
    Bienvestido 13
    Calistemon 19
    Cañafístola 23
    Cañandonga 24
    Cardenal 25
    Carolina 26
    Casia Nodosa 27
    Framboyán 44
    Framboyán Amarillo 45
    Frijolillo 46
    Garbancillo 50
    Guacamaya 53
    Guayaba 55
    Júpiter 59
    Lirio 62
    Magnolia 68
    Majagua 69
    Orquídea Silvestre 74
    Palo Bobo 76
    Paraíso 77
    Piñón 81
    Reina de las Flores 86
    Roble Amarillo 87
    Roble de Yugo 88
    Roble Maquiligua 89
    Tulipán Africano 93
    Varía 94
    Vomitel Colorado 96
Trinitaria 16
tubers, Lirio Turco 65
Tulip Tree 93
Tulipán Africano 93
Tumbergia Azul 38
Tunbergia 38

Vanda 103
Varía 94
Varía Negra 94
Varía Prieta 94
Vellosita 67
Vicaria 95
Vicaria Blanca 95
vines
    Aguinaldo Amarillo 3
    Aguinaldo Blanco 4
    Alamanda 6
    Corallilo 32

Fausto 38
Flor de Nieve 42
Jazmín de la Tierra 57
Lluvia De Orquídeas 66
Marrullero 72
Ojo de Poeta 73
Petrea 80
Piscuala 82
Violetina 50
Viuda 39, 73

Vomitel 96
Vomitel Colorado 96

Water Lily 75
Wedelia 90
White Cedar 89
White Ginger Lily 71
White Nightshade 42
White Water Lily 75
Wild Banana 84
Wild Cotton 7

Wild Jasmine 47
Wild Vine 72
Wind Flower 17

Yellow Bell 6
Yellow Flamboyant 45
Yellow Morning Glory 3
Yellow Poui 87
Yellow Shrimp Plant 29
Yucca 36
Yuramira 79

Index of Scientific names

Acalypha hispida 85
Acanthaceae 10, 29, 38,
 42, 67, 73, 91
Agavaceae 36
Allamanda cathartica 6
Alliaceae 5
Alpinia purpurata 8
Alpinia speciosa 30
Alpinia zerumbet 30
Amaryllidaceae 17, 64, 92
Angelonia pilosella 39
Anthurium andraeanum 9
Antigonon leptopus 32
Apocynaceae 2, 6, 62,
 63, 95
Araceae 9
Asteraceae 34, 41, 90
Asystasia gangetica 10
Azadirachta indica 77

Bauhinia galpinii 12
Bauhinia spp. 74
Beloperone gutata 29
Bignoniaceae 58, 87, 88,
 89, 93
Bixa orellana 14
Bixaceae 14
Bletia purpúrea 98
Bombax ellipticum 26
Boraginaceae 94, 96
Bougainvillea glabra 16
Broughtonia cubensis 100
Brugmansia x candida 20
Brunfelsia cestroides 49
Brunfelsia nitida 48

Cactaceae 1
Caesalpinia pulcherrima
 53
Caesalpiniaceae 12, 23,
 24, 25, 27, 44, 45, 53,
 54, 74
Calliandra
 haematocephala 18
Calliandra surinamensis
 18
Callistemon citrinus 19
Callistemon hortensis 19
Callistemon lanceolatus
 19

Callistemon speciosus 19
Canna spp. 83
Cannaceae 83
Cassia alata 54
Cassia fistula 23
Cassia grandis 24
Cassia javanica 27
Cassia nodosa 27
Catharanthus roseus 95
Cattleya labiata 99
Cestrum diurnum 47
Clerodendron x speciosum
 28
Cochlospermaceae 76
Cochlospermum vitifolium
 76
Combretaceae 82
Combretum indicum 82
Compositae 34, 41, 90
Congea tomentosa 66
Convolvulaceae 3, 4, 15,
 21, 40, 72
Cordia gerascanthus 94
Cordia sebestena 96
Cosmos spp. 34
Costus speciosus 22

Delonix regia 44
Duranta erecta 50
Duranta repens 50

Erythrina spp. 81
Euphorbia milii 33
Euphorbia pulcherrima 43
Euphorbiaceae 31, 33, 43,
 79, 85

Fabaceae 13, 46, 81

Galphimia glauca 52
Gardenia jasminoides 51
Gliricidia sepium 13
Gossypium spp. 7

Hebestigma cubense 46
Hedychium coronarium 71
Heliconia spp. 84
Heliconiaceae 84
Hemerocallis fulva 65
Hibiscus elatus 69
Hibiscus rosa-sinensis 70

Hibiscus schizopetalus 37
Hippeastrum puniceum 92
Hymenocallis latifolia 64

Ipomoea alba 40
Ipomoea carnea, subsp.
 fistulosa 21
Ipomoea crassicaulis 21
Ipomoea pes-caprae,
 subsp. *brasiliensis* 15
Ipomoea tiliacea 3, 72
Ixora coccinea 56
Ixora grandifolia 56
Ixora lutea 56
Ixora thwaitessi 56

Jasminum grandiflorum 57
Jatropha integerrima 79
Jatropha podagrica 31

Lagerstroemia indica 59
Lagerstroemia speciosa 86
Lamiaceae 28, 66
Leguminosae 12, 13, 18,
 23, 24, 25, 27, 44, 45,
 46, 53, 54, 74, 81
Liliaceae 65
Lythraceae 59, 86

Magnolia grandiflora 68
Magnoliaceae 68
Malpighiaceae 52
Malvaceae 7, 26, 37, 69, 70
Melia azedarach 77
Meliaceae 77
Merremia umbellata 3
Mimosaceae 18
Myrtaceae 19, 55

Nerium oleander 2
Nyctaginaceae 16
Nymphaea ampla 75
Nymphaea oderata 75
Nymphaea rosea 75
Nymphaeaceae 75

Oleaceae 57
Orchidaceae 97–103

Pachstachys lutea 29
Peltophorum pterocarpum
 45

Pentas lanceolata 78
Pereskia zinniflora 1
Petrea volubilis 80
Phaius tankervilliae 101
Phyllocarpus septentrionalis 25
Plumbaginaceae 35
Plumbago capensis 35
Plumeria clusioides 63
Plumeria rubra 62
Polygonaceae 32
Pseudobombax ellipticum 26
Psidium guajava 55

Quisqualis indica 82

Rhodocactus cubensis 1
Rubiaceae 51, 56, 78
Ruellia tuberosa 91

Russelia equisetiformis 60

Scrophulariaceae 39, 60
Senna alata 54
Solanaceae 20, 47, 48, 49, 61
Solanum havanense 61
Spathodea campanulata 93
Spathoglottis plicata 102
Strelitzia nicolai 11
Strelitzia reginae 11
Strelitziaceae 11

Tabebuia angustata 88
Tabebuia chrysantha 87
Tabebuia heterophylla 89
Tabebuia pentaphylla 89
Tagetes erecta 41
Talipariti elatum 69

Tecomaria capensis 58
Thryallis glauca 52
Thunberghia alata 73
Thunbergia erecta 67
Thunbergia fragrans 42
Thunbergia grandiflora 38
Tulbaghia violacea 5
Turbina corymbosa 4

Vanda teres 103
Verbenaceae 50, 80
Vinca rosea 95

Wedelia trilobata 90

Yucca aloifolia 36

Zephyranthes spp. 17
Zingiberaceae 8, 22, 30, 71

112